High·
Trust
LEADERSHIP

*A Proven System for Developing
an Organization of High-Performance
Financial Professionals*

D1113973

High· Trust
LEADERSHIP

A Proven System for Developing an Organization of High-Performance Financial Professionals

BILL NORMAN
BACHRACH LEVINE

Aim High
PUBLISHING

SAN DIEGO, CALIFORNIA

Aim High Publishing
8380 Miramar Mall, Suite 233
San Diego, CA 92121

First edition 1999

Designed and typeset by Robert Mott & Associates • Keswick, Virginia
Illustrated by Tom Klare • San Diego, California
Edited by Just Write • Keswick, Virginia
Printed in the United States of America

ISBN: 1-887006-02-8

Given the current legal environment, we suggest you have the forms offered
in this book reviewed by your compliance or legal advisors. We have not
intentionally included any advice or materials that put you at risk, but we
also realize how quickly and often laws and regulations change regarding
our industry.

OTHER BOOKS:

BY BILL BACHRACH
  *Values-Based Selling: The Art of Building High-Trust Client
    Relationships for Financial Advisors, Insurance
    Agents and Investment Reps*

BY NORMAN LEVINE
  Yes, You Can!

  How to Build a $100,000,000 Agency

  From Life Insurance to Diversification

  Selling With Silk Gloves, Not Brass Knuckles

  The Norman Levine Reader

Dedicated to
the growth, progress,
and success of
free enterprise.

NORMAN LEVINE

I dedicate this book to three of
my mentors: Ward Hanigan,
Doug Carter, and Max Dixon.
You have inspired me more than
you will ever know. Since it
would be impossible for me to
ever repay you for what you have
done for me, I will do my best to
"pay forward." I hope the content
of this book helps enough people
to make a dent in that debt.
Thank you.

BILL BACHRACH

CONTENTS

Introduction ix

1.
The Changing of the Guard:
Why *Leading* Is Replacing *Managing*
as the Key to the Future 1

2.
The Non-Interview:
Using a Career-Critical Social Skill
in Non-Business Settings. 19

3.
The Values Conversation:
Laying the Foundation of Trust
in Ten Minutes or Less 37

4.
Five Easy Steps:
Mastering the Values Conversation 57

5.
The Success Road Map:
Inspiring Producers to Succeed for Their Own Reasons 69

6.
The Groundwork of Greatness:
Developing Relationships to
Move Producers to the Next Level 103

7.
The High-Trust Culture:
Creating and Protecting an Environment for Success 127

8.
Beyond Goal Setting:
Helping Producers Build Themselves
as You Build Your Business 137

9.
The Seventh Generation:
Coaching to Win. 159

Resources and Author Information 175

Introduction

The purpose of this book is to help you create and implement some simple, proven strategies for hiring and retaining highly effective, happy producers who execute a smart, long-term business model. To make that happen, you must become the kind of leader who truly runs the organization, not just with a computer terminal and statistics, but with heart. You may have to rethink some of your beliefs and make some changes in your perceptions, your terminology, and your behavior.

Most producers and managers recognize that what their clients really want is a trusted advisor and not a salesperson, yet financial plans are frequently sold like just another product. As a result, many are only partially implemented. The financial plan is just another expensive toy, like the exercise bike that sits in the garage. When clients purchase plans this way, they have little or no use for them. They can't even hang laundry on them like they can on their exercise bikes. Have we done much more than create a culture of salespeople pretending to be financial planners? And you can be sure that more than one compliance department is wondering about the liability of an unimplemented written financial plan sitting on the credenza of a salesperson/financial planner.

Does this mean that your company or you, as a leader, should abandon delivering what the market really wants: a full-service financial advisor who is focused on helping the client? Of course not. It does mean that you are going to have to recruit differently, motivate differently, train differently, coach differently, and expect different behavior than you have before. What made you and others in your company successful in the past may be exactly the behavior that creates failure in the future. Take our own motto to heart: Past performance is no guarantee of future results. Just because the managers in Cleveland are posting big numbers, you may not want to emulate them. You are going to have to rise to a level of leadership that inspires your producers to rise to a level of uncommon loyalty.

The good news is that the strategies explained in this book create huge production, happy producers, and, most important, ecstatic clients who will do all of their business with one advisor and actually do all of the prospecting and marketing for that advisor, too.

Our book is for leaders and managers who are responsible for building and developing high-performance, highly productive groups of financial professionals who do

- financial planning
- investment management
- estate planning
- charitable planning and giving
- risk management

and who use securities and insurance products and services to help their clients achieve their goals. They are compensated by fee only, commission only, fee and commission, retainer, etc., which is determined by the individual producer and/or the company they represent or the manager or leader they are influenced by. Regardless of the type of compensation, the relationship or the processes are the same or similar for all financial professionals.

If this book is for leaders and not producers, why have this much discussion about producers? Because producers are *your* clients, and to lead them, you have to know them: the truth about where they are now, where they are going, what they are thinking, and what they are feeling. You have to understand their values and relate to their goals, dreams, and aspirations—genuinely care about being their leader. You have to care about them at least as much as you expect them to care about their clients.

We have written this book for a select group of individuals who know that you do not *manage* an organization into greatness; you must *lead* it. This implies you are competent, confident, and prepared to give your producers what they need to succeed. It also implies you are in a position to set an example, to "model" the behaviors you will ask of your producers. With this in mind, many chapters in this book offer skills that are directly translatable to client contacts. In other words, as you use these skills in leading your producers, you are actually showing them how to behave with clients. In addition, the Non-Interview presented in Chapter 2, the Values Conversation in Chapters 3 and 4, and the Success Road Map® in Chapter 5 are not only easily convertible for your producers, but they have already been successfully used by thousands of financial professionals. How producers can use the Values Conversation and a Success Road Map is explained in *Values-Based Selling: The Art of Building High-Trust Client Relationships for Financial Advisors, Insurance Agents and Investment*

Reps, and further reading on the Non-Interview can be found in *Selling With Silk Gloves, Not Brass Knuckles*.

The savvy leader already knows that the key to success today is not pricing, product selection, rates of return, or knocking the competition. *It is relationships.* Those who focus on the former rather than the latter not only end up with producers making fewer and smaller sales, they also flirt with ethical and compliance issues. Perhaps at the very worst, they influence producers to neglect or fall short of meeting clients' wants.

For skillful professionals, this opens the door to tremendous opportunities. Most consumers may never have met a financial professional who actually cares about them, is knowledgeable, and performs well in strategizing and problem solving. Indeed, many in the marketplace do not believe an advisor like this exists. While a huge amount of lip service has been paid to the importance of the relationship, there is very little real training on how to create one. How much trust training have your producers had? We believe our industry must return to basic competencies based on high-touch, relationship-oriented professionalism, while using modern technology and products for the creation of client-specific strategies, rather than as a basis for sales.

Likewise, the leader has tremendous opportunities to capitalize not only on a highly sophisticated pool of potential producers, but also on the void created by those who insist on managing instead of leading. There are those in the industry who, either by their own design or an inability to see beyond current pressures, have stuck their heads in the sand and not yet seen the wisdom of focusing on producers over the particulars of management.

Because you are reading this now, you are obviously already more focused on leadership than management. This does not mean you neglect compliance, cost controls, or any of the rest of it—just that you know what your priorities are. This book is designed to do one thing: help you help your producers.

We hope to inspire you and your team of producers to the next level. No matter what you have done in the past, no matter how accomplished you are already, a commitment to excellence demands that you continue to find new, better ways of serving your clients and guiding your producers to lifelong, lucrative careers with your organization. This is what high-trust leadership is doing for others. This is what it can do for you.

CHAPTER 1

The Changing of the Guard:
Why *Leading* Is Replacing *Managing* as the Key to the Future

> Leaders are *made*, they are not born, and they are made like everything else has been made in this country—by hard effort. And that's the price that we all have to pay to achieve that goal, or any goal.
>
> V I N C E   L O M B A R D I

We saw a bumper sticker the other day: IF YOU REMEMBER THE SIXTIES YOU WEREN'T THERE! Well, we were both there and haven't entirely forgotten those heady days. It wasn't just "flower power" and tie-dyed T-shirts versus the "establishment" and pin-striped suit crowd. Think about what people could count on then: the Soviet Union, Studebaker, silver coins, ten-cent hamburgers, house calls, and mimeographs. Gone are those cultural icons; none play a part in our lives today. In fact, you may not remember them at all. Now we rely on cable TV, cellular phones, e-mail, the Internet, NASDAQ, Starbucks, baby monitors, and ATMs. Remarkably, today's necessities didn't even exist a mere two generations ago. As another bumper sticker says, SHIFT HAPPENS.

Everywhere we turn, someone tells us how great change is, how we must embrace it and see the opportunities it holds. So many management books quote John F. Kennedy about how the Chinese word for crisis incorporates the characters for both danger and opportunity that the idea no longer captures our attention. Even crisis has become passé.

All the experts are blabbing about reinventing this and reorganizing that. Yet, for the rest of us, accepting change day-to-day can be daunting. At least one thing we hear is true: The rate of change is only speeding up. The world is flying by, and the only safe prediction is that paradigm shifts and technological revolutions will continue to reach into our lives and shake us by the collar, make us think on our feet, and take us to new, often better ways of doing business.

For the financial services industry, recent decades brought massive, lightning-quick consolidation and completely changed the rules of the game. Even the term *financial services* didn't exist before the eighties. More important, once-large profits shrank dramatically while the available labor pool expanded, so we were forced to hire more selectively. Consumers have a much wider range of places from which to purchase investments—their bank, insurance or payroll companies, a full-service financial firm. They can even access a broker or agent from their home via the Internet. In fact, investors can place trade orders twenty-four hours a day with the new technology, and at discounted commission charges as little as 15% of traditional fees. Consumers can buy *all* of the available investments and insurance products *without* a broker or agent, or from many different advisors.

WHAT HAPPENED?
How Consolidation Affected the Financial Services Industry

Consolidation is the watchword for any highly competitive industry. The banking world is a good example. In the early eighties and before, you could pay a visit to a small, hometown bank: a center of social activity, possibly owned by your neighbors and staffed by tellers and loan officers you knew and trusted. The little bank made money for its investors and opened branches throughout the area.

Suddenly, your little bank was gobbled up by a bigger bank. Things changed overnight. The name, the logo, your checks, and the procedures you'd followed for years changed in a flash.

Consolidation did the same thing to the financial services industry. A number of factors led to the massive change in the eighties and early nineties. In his introduction to *The Financial Services Revolution,* editor Clifford Kirsch sums up the dramatic change: "Workers who were once promised a set pension are today responsible for investing their own retirement money. Money management, once the prerogative of only the very wealthy, is now increasingly available to middle-class households through their participation in mutual funds and other investment vehicles. More now than ever before, individuals are no longer just savers, they are investors."

The very roles of our investment institutions changed. Banks, insurance companies, and mutual funds broke out of the roles they once played. According to conventional wisdom once upon a time, banks were for checking and savings accounts, insurance companies were to protect against risk, and mutual funds were for pooling your investment dollars into a single vehicle.

Today banks offer investment services that run the gamut

(continued next page)

and insurance companies have their own mutual funds. Wirehouse brokerage firms offer money market funds, checking accounts, credit cards, loans, and so on. This, combined with consumers' new sophistication, has created a shopping mentality, the *financial services industry* has been born, and all hell has broken loose. Welcome to the twenty-first century.

The best thing to come from consolidation was the marked end of the *salesperson* era and the beginning of the age of the *trusted advisor.* If you were going to prosper in the new financial services game you were going to be versatile, agile, and cover all the bases—a real multipurpose advisor. The salesperson was the guy who found out what you didn't have, then reached into his bag of products to sell it to you—or poked around until he found a "wound" or "disturbed" you enough to buy. The trusted advisor is the person who becomes so important to and trusted by the client that he or she is consulted before any investment/insurance choice is made. In fact, the trusted advisor is the single source consulted for all financial strategies and products: diagnosis, a written strategy, and systematic implementation.

This shift is right in line with a Stanford Research Institute survey of the industry. Conducted in the eighties, it showed that the majority of consumers questioned were confused by the array of products dished out by persons from competing financial institutions, whose advice was often contradictory. The respondents also stated they preferred one person to be their expert advisor to assess their overall financial requirements and shepherd them through the strategies, going so far as to assemble a team of experts when necessary. They wanted someone who cared enough to get to know them on a personal level and respond to their needs and wants. Today, that "someone" is in your organization working for you. And wanting the same thing from you, their leader, that their clients want from them: a high-trust relationship.

This consolidation and emphasis on technological advances brought with it a fair amount of distractive power, frequently diverting managers' focus from recruiting and helping people produce—the only two functions that can't be performed by a clerk or computer. Instead, managers were forced further into the compliance arena as companies diversified; they became more involved with cost controls, budgeting, and basic administration as margins dried up. They used to do everything with a pencil and a pad of paper; now it's with a digital assistant. Today's technology—computers, databases, phone systems, and the electronic organizer—demands constant updating in the race against obsolescence, which means constant revisions to training procedures. Distraction feeds distraction. It's too easy to get caught up in the drudge work and dragged away from the only two things that make you any money: recruiting and cultivating a high-performance, high-trust team of financial professionals. The bottom line? To succeed today, you must become a leader and not merely a manager.

Managers ensure there is a place to work, a procedure to follow, and a system for monitoring business. Leaders, on the other hand, build high-performance teams by focusing on interpersonal relationships with producers, guiding them to achieve their dreams and aspirations. Everything else is minutiae that should be delegated to someone else or relegated to after hours. *A leader makes the relationship with producers the first priority.*

While we don't have a crystal ball to see exactly what the future will hold, we do know this—the future of the financial services industry requires great leaders, not only at the company level but, more important, in the field. While we think CEOs will love this book, it is written for the *hands-on leader in the field.* There is a need for leaders who will interpret the necessity of hiring selectively as a catalyst for hiring not just fewer but *better* people, who will find those potential top producers and give them what they need to succeed. These men and women will operate in a new environment that leaves little room for mediocrity and no room for failure.

The future of the financial services industry requires great leaders, not only at the company level but, more important, in the field.

This book proceeds from a simple assumption: *The best success formula for financial services in the twenty-first century is to have trusted advisors guided by trusted leaders.* This is a far cry from salespeople supervised by managers. Simply put, producers will do things for leaders they trust that they won't do for anyone else. Indeed, all financial professions have at least one thing in common: The high-trust relationship is the key not only to producers' success with clients, but also to leaders' success with producers. Just as the people in your organization are making the shift from transaction-oriented salespeople to trusted financial advisors, now you must make the transition from task-oriented manager to trusted leader. Of course, this presupposes that you really are a trustworthy leader with the system and skills to help producers be successful. Is that true? If it is, then you can go right to work recruiting and developing your high-trust, high-performance team. If it is not yet true, then you will need to get to work developing yourself.

WHAT IF NORMAN SPENT THE DAY WITH YOU?

Many, many years ago, early in my management career, I began to show significant progress. The company recognized me as a future star and began to give me a great deal of encouragement and some public acknowledgment. At about the same time, a good friend was appointed manager for the same company. His record was not very impressive. I knew him to be a hard worker, but he was not adding many good people and those he did add weren't producing. In contrast, our organization was adding people faster than any other agency in the company, and our average per-capita production was the highest in the company. Eventually, this other manager called and asked if I would come visit to see if I could figure out what he was doing or not doing that was causing him to have this very unimpressive production record. I told him yes, but I wouldn't give him my impressions until the end of the day; I'd just watch.

(continued next page)

We spent an entire day together, starting with breakfast and ending long after the sun went down. Here's what struck me: His day was totally different from mine. After breakfast, he went into the office and checked his morning mail. He went to the administrative section to make sure everything was being appropriately handled, that the paperwork and the details were being effectively managed. He went back to his office and began to work on some promotional material. Soon the morning was half gone and he had not really talked to a single production-oriented person. The rest of the day wasn't much different.

He did all of the jobs a clerk/manager might do and none of the jobs that a personal leader ought to do. At the end of the day, I had to tell him: "The biggest difference between us is I spend my entire day, from 8 A.M. until 6 P.M., with people. I visit with them, and I try to help them be productive. I figured out a long time ago that if I help them achieve their goals, I achieve mine. I spend my time getting them to produce. I motivate them, I teach them, I train them, and I work with them. I touch them and try to be there when they need a friend. You're spending all of your time doing paperwork and administration. I think your office is a lot more efficient than mine, but mine clearly is a great deal more effective. I can hire people to do what you're doing and I can trust the people who work for me and even allow them to make mistakes in the clerical and administrative area more easily than I can afford to neglect the people who are producing the business."

I suggested to him that he spend his days with people and his evenings and his weekends with paper, and stop spending so much time doing what I consider the defensive parts of the business. It wasn't an overnight turnaround, but eventually he began to run a pretty good agency, and then was promoted to a vice president's position in the home office.

What would I find if I came and spent the day with you?

—NORMAN LEVINE

No matter how many times our industry gets turned upside down or inside out—no matter how many new products, circumstances, laws, rules, regulations, or economic factors are thrown into the mix—the fundamental principles of leadership endure. Although the "high touch" aspect of financial services was put aside for a time while all eyes were on "high tech," much of what we advocate in this book has been around for decades. In the old days, managers hadn't perfected interpersonal skills, but they held them paramount. The important concern now is how to get these skills back and update them for today's leaders and producers. Two management objectives rise from the fray: high trust and high performance.

In this book, we'll give you the best of both worlds: the principles of a leader who has been in the business for more than fifty years and built several multimillion-dollar organizations, as well as step-by-step processes for creating high-trust relationships from one of financial services' foremost opinion leaders. We are from different generations and different branches of the financial industry, but the root of what we teach is the same: High trust equals high performance. Together we bring you two perspectives—one of a highly respected career insurance man and the other of a successful producer turned coach to top producers and management—that together yield practical, expert advice.

◆ **We will provide you with methods, not "techniques."**

For example, the Non-Interview and Values Conversation models in the next three chapters provide you with proven processes for establishing and enhancing relationships with your producers. This will ultimately lead them to perform at their highest level for you, as well as secure their loyalty. Unlike trendy, cookie-cutter management tools that leave your people feeling "techniqued," the Non-Interview and Values Conversation begin with the presumption that you are a leader who takes a personal interest in the people who work with you. As such, we are not promoting a new approach for manipulating candidates into accepting a position with your firm or for squeezing one more production hour or sale out of a failing new-hire. Although we provide you with sample dialogues, this book is not about memorizing a set of scripts. You can learn the capitals of all fifty states by rote, but until you've been there, you won't know Boston from Baton Rouge. Likewise, this book is about "going there" and bringing back the practical interpersonal skills that will take you to the future that both you and your producers desire and deserve.

◆ **We focus on interpersonal skills over "management skills."**

It is a given that you will have training and group meetings, that you will set annual goals and write plans for attaining them, and that you will role-play with your producers and meet with them periodically. There are a number of other books written on these rudiments of management, so we have not covered that old ground here. Instead, the emphasis is on such crucial leadership abilities as listening and coaching, your style of leading, and inspiring producers to be successful for their own reasons.

◆ **We'll answer some key questions facing leaders of financial services companies today.**

All of these issues will be addressed individually and throughout the book:

1. *Profitability.* How do I get people to develop the high-trust relationships that produce profitable business that stays on the books?

2. *Productivity.* How do I get more business than I've ever gotten before?

3. *Recruiting.* How do I find quality people? How do I attract them and help them become part of the organization?

4. *Retaining.* How do I keep quality people once they've joined me?

5. *Mergers and acquisitions.* How will I be affected in the case of a merger or acquisition?

6. *Diversification.* How can I keep my focus on the people with the demands for knowledge and technical expertise of diversification?

7. *Competition.* How do I outproduce my competition? Should I even be concerned with my competition?

8. *Market.* How do my producers get quality clients in today's world?

9. *Client relationships.* How do we develop solid client relationships and provide caring service?

Adapt or Die

In this book you will learn to implement high-trust leadership in building a successful financial service organization. High-trust leaders are bold, confident individuals who gamely throw away the archaic system of *managing people* along with their old 286 PCs and adopt the innovative practice of meaningful leadership. Like the buggy whip salesman who, upon seeing the first automobile roll by, bought a car franchise, these new leaders will adapt quickly and pull vision, reason, clarity, and success out of the confusion. Those who adapted just following the shake-up of the eighties became more successful and were more rewarded than anyone ever has been in the history of our industry. You have the same opportunity now.

The key will be *selection.* Any leader who wants to effectively run a client- and results-oriented organization must develop the capacity to select the right people, which is a skill unto itself and the direct result of listening, being sensitive, and finding out what motivates people rather than trying to force them to fit a mold. You can't afford to do what was done in decades past: hire so many people just to find one successful producer. You have to be smarter about it, hire better people, and create the right environment to keep them.

ON BEING SELECTIVE

There's an old philosophy in the insurance and securities industries that you "sell the career," implying that you convince people with potential that this is a career they ought to consider: They would be more successful, they'd have more freedom, they'd make more money, they'd have more control of their own destiny. Yadda, yadda, yadda. Then there's the "selling of the company": They ought to work with you because your company is better than the other company.

But that's backwards. The wrong person is doing the selling.

Shouldn't it be your candidates? After all, if they can't sell you on how and why they are going to be a blue-chip investment of your time and money, how will they ever be able to handle the prospecting and selling required in financial services? If they can't build a relationship of trust with you, how will they ever do that effectively in a skeptical marketplace? Are they the kind of people to whom you would entrust your own and your family's financial future? If not, why would you send them out to do that for other people and their families?

Let them "sell" you: "We have a process or a method that is guaranteed to produce great results, provided you follow it. Convince me, the leader of this great organization, why I should invest my limited and valuable time, energy, and resources with you instead of somebody else."

When you begin the recruiting/selection process with candidates, you are creating an opportunity to help them have whatever kind of life they want: to meet their needs, achieve their goals, and fulfill their values. Since we believe that trust is the key to success in this business, that's where we suggest you focus first— not on "convincing strategies." And the truth is that you build trust by listening to their story, not by telling yours.

—BILL BACHRACH

Traditionally, there have been three types of producers. We're sure you've seen all of them in your organization.

◆ The first group is comprised of those who, for whatever reason, will fail in this business no matter what you do. Perhaps they're not driven or motivated sufficiently; they may not have the skills or talent. Regardless, *you cannot help them succeed.*

◆ The second group is so proactive and self-disciplined that you have to do little or nothing for them, and these producers will still succeed in spades. Yet the challenge with this group is that if you attempt to *manage* them and cannot keep the attention and loyalty of this group, they will be lost to a real *leader.* For them, a manager can be useful but is not essential to success.

◆ The third group is coachable. They're not naturals; they have limited God-given talent, but with coaching they do extremely well. A leader is the key. Without the proper training and motivation, these producers will probably fail, but with the proper direction they can become central to the success of your organization.

We'll look further at identifying who is who in the next few chapters, but for now let's stay with the obvious: In selecting people for your organization, you want to focus on the second and third groups. (Apparent though this may be, no doubt you are like most executives who have "invested in someone's potential" only to be disappointed. Maybe the thing to do is quit investing in people's potential and start concentrating on those whose *reality* is to be successful.) The key to attracting and keeping people from these two groups is the high-trust relationship, and the ability to form such relationships is the distinguishing characteristic between a leader and a manager. The interpersonal aspects of the relationship—*What's important to you? How do you feel? Do you have problems? How can I help, be your buddy, mentor, friend, confidante, coach?*—are what make the difference. If you can establish that kind of relationship with the people in your organization, they're not going to leave just because someone else offers them a better payout, a six-figure signing bonus, a secretary, or a corner office. However, if you don't have that kind of relationship, you can expect to lose them to the highest bidder.

The key to attracting and keeping people from these two groups is the high-trust relationship, and the ability to form such relationships is the distinguishing characteristic between a leader and a manager.

It's like the difference between your doctor and your pharmacist. Generally, the pharmacist dispenses directions and the product you requested. If there is a competing pharmacy with the same or better products for less, you'd change pharmacists, wouldn't you? With no personal touch, why would you feel any loyalty? Yet your doctor holds a different position. He or she is your trusted health expert and advisor, and you expect a certain bedside manner, care, and concern that make this doctor *your* doctor. You may get a prescription (and you can trot off to the best-priced pharmacy), but when you have a health concern, you want someone who really cares about you and knows how to help you improve your health, even if it's already good.

Here's an interesting question: How do you know how good your doctor really is? Every doctor has diploma after diploma hanging on the wall. They all have medical books and charts, white coats, stethoscopes, and tongue depressors, but how do you know if they are any good at being a doctor? If you're like most people you rely on that bedside manner—how the doctor treats you as a person.

Being a good leader in the financial services industry requires many of the same characteristics as being a good doctor. You have to listen to those you lead, diagnose their needs and wants, and provide a strategy for optimal health by providing the right kind of environment for them to achieve those goals. To do all of this *you must be trusted on a personal level.* Therefore, building that trust is the most important thing you can do to become a successful organization builder. How much trust training have you had? It would be unusual if you could say that you'd had any. That's why you're reading this book: No more leaving the most important aspect of interpersonal relationships to chance—we're going to build trust on purpose.

Financial Services Organizations of the Future

We truly believe the outlook for financial service businesses is the best it's ever been. Never before in history have there been so many people making so much money and with so much need and desire for help in making smart choices about their money. One impressive statistic has baby boomers becoming heirs and heiresses to trillions of dollars in their lifetimes. The demand for financial professionals is unbelievable, and the potential for those who stick with it and become qualified professionals is also unbelievable. We can look forward with great optimism to the future and recognize that the good old days, which may have seemed great, were nothing like what's going to happen tomorrow.

We must simply remember what business we're in. At the risk of being lumped in with other management books, we'll borrow one of their popular analogies: If the railroad companies had realized they were in the transportation business rather than the railroad business, they would by now control the trucking industry, the airlines, and every other form of transportation. Instead, they hung onto being in the train business. Whether they thought that would continue forever or they were just stubborn isn't the point; they made a mistake leaders of this industry won't.

We're in the people/financial problem-solving and strategizing business. We're also trying to help people keep their career commitments. As a leader, once you've selected your producers, your job is to help them achieve their goals, wants, and dreams so they experience more values fulfillment. Trying to force a round peg into a square hole will not work. In the next three chapters of this book, we'll focus on two methodologies, one for meeting people and assessing business potential, and the other for screening candidates and creating trust in the first ten minutes of your first meeting.

Is it possible? Are there successful leaders out there who are building great relationships and who have a cadre of producers who are not only getting big results, but wouldn't think of going anywhere else? Yes. So, if others are doing that, why can't you? If you're willing to become someone who is excellent at building relationships and creating feelings of trust, we're confident that *you can*. It won't matter what happens to any system; it will not matter how much change, consolidation, or reorganization your company experiences. There is *always* room for a leader with a successful group of producers.

CHAPTER **2.**

The Non-Interview:
Using a Career-Critical Skill
in Non-Business Settings

> You can't make a silk purse
> out of a sow's ear.
>
> OLD APHORISM

The luck of the Irish may be the product of something a little more substantial. Until their galvanizing defeat on Easter Sunday in 1916, the forces seeking Irish independence from Great Britain had no luck at all. They'd been beaten in just about every attempt to oust the British for nearly five hundred years.

Enter Michael Collins, an accountant and rebel who had served some time in jail for it. "Mick," as he was known, believed if the Irish were ever to have their own independent state, they'd have to change the way they fought the British. Because he and his boyos were greatly outnumbered, outgunned, and out of money, instead of regular armies of parading men and women in proper uniforms, Collins organized the ragtag volunteers into "flying columns." A handful of men and women waged a guerrilla war against the largest military force in the world as they conducted successful campaigns throughout the whole of Ireland with only a fraction of the numbers of the opposition. The key to the success of the Irish was not luck at all—it was *information.*

Mick Collins believed the Irish forces had to know everything about the British to beat them. His favorite tactic for gathering information was to ask questions of everyone he met on the streets of Dublin. Because the British had little information about him, Collins boldly rode around the city on a bicycle in a hat and pinstriped suit. He'd blithely stop for tea and ask the British officers sitting at the next table how things were going at Dublin Castle, the hub of British administration in Ireland. He'd attend formal balls and dinners and calmly ask the wives of British officers where their husbands were or had been recently. These unsuspecting people innocently answered his questions. Collins and his staff recorded the information, then linked it all together and used it to hold out against overwhelming odds and fight the British army to a standstill. What seemed like uninteresting trivia helped Mick Collins and the Irish rebels bring the British government to the bargaining table in 1921 for what was the first step in achieving Irish independence.

Although hiring the right people is not the same as fighting a war, it can mean the life or death of your organization. The process for selecting those people has traditionally been a cold one. Have you ever changed your natural voice, posture, and language when the selling hat went on? The same can be true of interviewing. Typical interviews usually end up strained and stiff. What can you possibly learn from a person who may be so nervous you can almost see the cue cards on which they've written answers to the same old canned questions? Because selection is so important to high-trust leadership, "strained and stiff" won't cut it. What we've designed is a way to sort the people you want to recruit before you actually recruit them. Successful leaders use their time efficiently and effectively, and once you know what type of person you want to add to your organization, this tool allows you the advantage of looking all the time without being obvious. What we're describing in this chapter is the first step in the secret of that success—the Non-Interview.*

Although the Non-Interview is ultimately a useful tool in recruiting, more important, it is simply a critical social skill. It is a way of interacting with people as you go about your day-to-day life that enhances your business when you aren't necessarily

---

The Non-Interview is a way of interacting with people as you go about your day-to-day life that enhances your business when you aren't necessarily doing business.

---

doing business. Being successful in a people-oriented profession requires lots of comfortable interactions with people, both in and out of the office. You can be at a Kiwanis Club meeting, in line at the supermarket, or at a planned informal meeting over a cup of coffee—your first contact, the first time you meet someone, *can always be a Non-Interview.* It can take as little as five minutes or as long as all day. The amount

---

*The Non-Interview process was originally written about in Norman Levine's *Selling With Silk Gloves, Not Brass Knuckles* and is explained in detail for producers in the tape series "If You Sell Well, There Are No Impossible Dreams." For more information on this and other products, please see the back of this book.

of time you spend will be a judgment call based on the level of your personal relationship and how much time you want to invest.

The Non-Interview is exactly what the name implies—a visit that is not, nor does it look or feel like, a formal interview. Think about attending a dinner party at a friend's house. Before the evening is over you will have a comfortable rapport with one or more of the guests. When you meet again there will be immediate recognition and friendliness. On the other hand, there will be people at the dinner you won't even remember the next day. The rapport you achieve with the one or two people results from the chemistry you find while Non-Interviewing them. That's the way friendships are formed, and that's the way finding producers will work. You have to Non-Interview

people to find the right chemistry you need to create a successful organization. Obviously, this part of the relationship can't be a memorized track. To be good at the Non-Interview you must develop communication skills that are uniquely you. No two Non-Interviews will ever be exactly alike.

The key to the Non-Interview is getting *other people* to talk. It can be done in minutes or in many visits, over eighteen holes of golf or during a social evening with new acquaintances. The Non-Interview encourages someone to share his or her dreams and aspirations and helps get answers to questions that determine if and how to pursue a personal or business relationship. If you do this six times a day, thirty times

During the Non-Interview, you let the other person do the talking.

a week, with different people—not with the intent to recruit them, but with the idea of *getting to know* them—you will have four positive results: 1) you'll meet a lot of nice people, 2) you'll become even more proficient at listening and eventually develop the ability not only to hear people's responses but to "read" their body language, to intuit what other people are thinking and feeling, 3) you'll hone your ability to discern who might be interested in and benefit from a career with you, and 4) you'll enlarge the "pond" in which you fish for excellent candidates, thus allowing you to become truly selective.

TIPS FOR CONDUCTING AN EFFECTIVE NON-INTERVIEW

Be relaxed, non-adversarial, informal, and listen a lot . . . much, much more than you talk.

- Listen with your eyes; pay attention to body language.

- Communicate with interest, concern, and compatibility.

- Do not sell or recruit.

Once you've become proficient at the Non-Interview, you may find it is more of a sorting process than one of selection because different people will be suited for different roles in your life. During the Non-Interview, a leader will answer three questions that serve to pre-select the potential candidate from the many other new acquaintances.

Q: Is this a person with whom I want any kind of relationship? If there's no personal interest or chemistry, there is no need to proceed. Don't waste time trying to fit square pegs into round holes. You wouldn't try to persuade someone to become your friend under these circumstances; don't consider recruiting producers this way, either.

Q: *If I decide to proceed with a business relationship, when should I do it?* If the contact is at a social event, it may not be appropriate to launch into a more formal interview yet. Of course, if the circumstances are correct, you may proceed with a more specific interview. In most situations, it is better to arrange another appointment at a more suitable time and place.

Q: *What can I learn from this person?* Successful people have plenty to teach the rest of the world. Whether this is ultimately a person you want to add to your organization or not, what can *you* learn from *them?*

Since the Non-Interview can often lead you to consider someone as a candidate, it means you have to listen. Listening is often referred to as the "lost art," and for good reason. Not many people can boast great listening skills today. But like Mick Collins and the Irish rebels, listening can give you the advantage you need to make better decisions. As the Non-Interview is a covert way of discovering the right people, the only way to do this is to ask question after question after question. The questions you ask should be designed to accomplish three things: determine if you like this person, let the person know you're good at what you do and you care about them, and find out what makes the person tick.

How do you determine whether you like someone? Although there are many reasons why you may like someone or not, the one foolproof method to finding out is to get the person talking and keep your own mouth shut as much as possible. Get people to talk about themselves, their family, their spouse or significant other, their kids—wherever they want to go with the conversation. You're looking for the right chemistry. And although chemistry is an intangible thing, you'll know it when you feel it. Would this person be a friend of yours? Would you have him or her over for dinner? Would you take his or her advice on a restaurant or movie?

SAMPLE NON-INTERVIEW

The Non-Interview is a fairly unstructured conversation driven by personality, circumstance, and what you discover while talking. Think of yourself as a skilled reporter who is able to do two things at once: stay focused on the other person and ask questions that move the conversation along seamlessly. Your questions either redirect in a subtle way or flow from the person's previous answer. Following is an example—not a script per se, but a demonstration of how one Non-Interview could proceed.

Leader. (*Using a transition appropriate to the circumstance*) **How delightful that we'd meet at such a great party. Our host says you are a terrific person, but I don't really know anything about you. What do you do for a living?**

Other. Oh, I'm a manager in a local biotech firm. Maybe you've heard of it? Bio-Company? (*continued next page*)

Leader.	Oh, sure. That sounds like a big time commitment . . .
Other.	It is.
Leader.	Do you have a family, too?
Other.	Yes, my wife and I have two kids.
Leader.	Wow, I bet balancing your job with family can be challenging.
Other.	Sometimes, yeah. What do you do?
Leader.	I lead a team of financial professionals—trusted advisors, really. We work pretty hard, too, but we love it and it's certainly rewarding. Do you love your career?
Other.	Well, I have a degree in accounting and this job is a pretty good fit with my skills. Plus it's close to home.
Leader.	Do you plan on doing this forever?
Other.	Maybe. It depends on what other opportunities come my way.
Leader.	Really? What are your dreams and aspirations?
Other.	What I'd really love to do is make enough money so that I can either retire early or work at my "real job" only half of the year. My secret passion is writing, but I know I can't support myself and my family with this—yet. *(Laughs.)* I'm no John Grisham.
Leader.	So you love to write. I'm a big reader, myself. What do you love about it?
Other.	It's creative and analytical all at once. What do you like to read?

Leader.	Mostly non-fiction, but I enjoy a good story every now and then. Do you get much of a chance to write these days?
Other.	Not really. My work is pretty structured and demanding. Not that I mind hard work—don't get me wrong. In fact, I like sinking my teeth into something big.
Leader.	Have you ever thought about going into a different profession to support your goal of writing more?
Other.	Not really.
Leader.	Would you be open to discussing it with me?
Other.	I'm not sure what you mean, but . . .
Leader.	I can see how you might be able to achieve your goals of early retirement or a more flexible work schedule without a drop in income. I realize this isn't the time or place, but if you'd like to give me your number, I'd be very interested in talking with you more.
Other.	Sure, I'll give you my number and we can have lunch.
Leader.	Yeah, that would be great anyway. I'd love to hear more about what you're writing or planning to write . . .

The Non-Interview always proceeds in this way, with the leader asking a lot of questions, listening, and volunteering only enough about himself or herself to keep the conversation rolling. The point is to let the other person talk; the more he or she says, the more

(continued next page)

you'll learn. When you feel the conversation is done, you should know to proceed in one of four directions: 1) no further effort: you don't have a real affinity for this person; 2) friendship: this is a person with whom you can socialize but not do business; 3) let's talk business: this is someone you would love to coach in a successful career with your organization; or 4) perhaps this could be a client for you or your firm.

In the example above, the person is a potential candidate, someone who has a reason to consider what you would offer and is comfortable in conversation. The foundation of trust has already been laid by the leader's attentiveness and the other person's openness about an important goal in life. If, however, it had gone something like this, the leader would simply bow out gracefully:

Leader.	*(Using a transition appropriate to the circumstance)* How delightful that we'd meet at such a great party. Our host says you are a terrific person, but I don't really know anything about you. What do you do for a living?
Other.	I'm a manager in a local biotech firm.
Leader.	Really, which one?
Other.	Bio-Company. What do you do?
Leader.	I lead a team of financial professionals—trusted advisors, really. How do you know our host?
Other.	We went to college together.
Leader.	Oh, yeah? That's great. What university?
Other.	UCLA. Go Bruins, you know?
Leader.	*(Laughs.)* What did you study?
Other.	Accounting.

Leader.	Did you like it?
Other.	Not really. But it pays the bills, so to speak.
Leader.	What do you do when you're not paying the bills? You look pretty athletic. Are you into sports?
Other.	Uh huh.
Leader.	Which ones?
Other.	You know, whatever. I work out.
Leader.	Is fitness very important to you?
Other.	Yeah.
Leader.	Oh, listen, I'm sorry to be abrupt, but I see an old friend I should say hello to. It's been nice talking to you.

Clearly, there is no chemistry in this conversation. If you have the time and the inclination, you can exhaust all subjects until you hit on something that excites the other person, but when things are puttering along at this lackluster pace, you may be better off to drop it and just chalk it up as one more Non-Interview under your belt.

Conduct the Non-Interview in restaurants, gas stations, at dry cleaners. Learn more about your doctor, dentist, attorney, and accountant. If the extent of your personal knowledge of these important people in your life is what their expertise and fees are, get busy. Do they live near the office? Are they married? Do they have kids? Who are their best friends? How long have they known one another? What's really important to them? If you conduct the Non-Interview thirty times a week, every week, you will not only have the pleasure of getting to know a wonderful and diverse mix of people, but you will also end up with a reservoir of valuable personal, social, and career experiences. The key to improving your interpersonal skills and having lots of people in your world is to become comfortable talking to everyone.

There's the story of the graduate student who began flying from Washington, D.C. to Dallas once each week as research for his thesis. His objective on the three-hour flight was to have a conversation with the person seated next to him. He'd start the conversation by asking a question and continue to subtly and unobtrusively ask questions for the entire flight. If he had to answer a question he'd do it in one quick sentence and get back to questioning his subject. After the flight two friends would be waiting at the airport in Dallas to interview the person he'd chosen as a subject. His results? The people he'd been seated with found him to be delightful, friendly, and one of the most interesting people they'd ever met. But none of them could remember any details about him: his name, where he lived, why he was flying to Dallas. Nothing. He was the most interesting person they'd ever met, but *they didn't know anything about him.* His conclusion? By allowing people to talk about themselves you become a much more trusted person. In fact, people may find you more interesting, which can be a good by-product of a Non-Interview.

Trust and strong personal relationships clearly begin at the initial greeting. Just go about the Non-Interview as any friendly person would—talk about the things that are important to the other person: special interests and hobbies, lifestyle, family, business success, type and length of career, charities, sports, politics. Obviously, you won't necessarily discuss all of these; you bring up only as many as needed to get you to a person's emotional "command center," the area that is so meaningful that they *want* to talk with you about it.

In the course of the conversation, let the person know you're successful. Brag, briefly (and with charm, if possible), about something you've done. Though most of the Non-Interview is listening, this is the short part where you get to tell the other person

---

Just go about the Non-Interview as any friendly person would—talk about the things that are important to the other person.

---

something about yourself. Make sure they know you're successful at what you do and that you care about the success of others, then let them talk.

Finally, finding out a person's emotional motives shouldn't be difficult. We all have them: taxes, hobbies, favorite causes, inflation, business, family, home, an unfulfilled desire. What is it that lights a fire in these people? What stirs them up? What are they passionate about? One key thing to look for here is whether *anything* fires them up. A person without a passion probably won't catch the world on fire when representing your organization.

In the Non-Interview, you're looking for the other person's dreams, goals, and wants. Since the Non-Interview is conducted without a pencil or pad of paper, the effective communicator listens and remembers an impression of what the person wants to accomplish and why it has not already been done.

Remember, this is *not* a job interview: You are simply having a casual conversation. You are looking to see if you are interested in this person first, whether he or she is interested in you, and whether you'd even consider a friendship. If you feel like you are selling or recruiting, you are not doing it right. You are not in "business mode" during the Non-Interview. What's more, you can't ask all the questions all the time, or you begin to sound like a tabloid reporter. Just get the conversation started, then keep it going until you feel comfortable with the person.

During this low-profile, nonadversarial Non-Interview, it's appropriate to share private information about both business and personal matters. Remember, you may have to open up a bit yourself. You can briefly recount what your dreams and desires were or are and how you systematically went about attaining them or are pursuing them today. Talking about yourself is only a bridge to get the other person talking. Listening is the key to understanding and recognizing what you're looking for. Also keep in mind that trust requires a strong relationship between the leader and those he or she leads, so you're looking for someone with whom you can begin a personal relationship.

Using the "M&Ms" to Recognize Potential Peak Performers

One of the primary benefits of the Non-Interview is that it gives the leader a chance to measure someone against the profile of a top producer. The following criteria, all starting with M so they're easy to remember while you're conducting a Non-Interview, provide a benchmark for selecting the right people.

1. *Morality.* Among the more important attributes is morality. Without proper ethics and principles, even if they managed to succeed in our industry, they could destroy it and should be kept out from the beginning. You want someone who has good work habits and no problem complying with rules, laws, and regulations.

2. Market. They need to have a market they can address once they come into the business, or they must have the capacity to develop one. If they have neither, they may fail in your organization. Ask yourself, *Is this person's market adequate, accessible, appropriate?* (If there is no established market and the person looks good in all other categories, consider whether the individual has the capacity because of existing skills or experience to create one.)

3. Marital stability. "Marital" may be a bit of misnomer, but it starts with M. The point is, it doesn't matter if someone is married, single, or if they have an unconventional relationship. In fact, in a formal interview setting, it's against the law to even ask the question, yet in a social context, the subject may come up. What matters to success is that they have *stability*. It is a disservice to you and the other person if you attempt to recruit someone who is at a time in their lives when they are more likely to fail. Never forget that intense interpersonal stress overpowers almost all other attributes during some part of most people's lives; this is not the time to begin a meaningful, new career. Look for someone who is in a position to make the most of this profession.

4. Mental attitude. Emotional and intellectual fitness are equally important. While you don't have to be a rocket scientist to succeed in this industry, you do have to be able to learn, think, and be responsive to people's needs and wants. Look for a positive mental attitude, organizational compatibility, and an eagerness to learn.

5. *Motivation.* If someone is not self-motivated, you'll have a problem. Everyone is born with a pilot light, but some people don't ever burn the main flame. As a matter of fact, some of them blow it out. What you need is someone who will overcome the bad days and inevitable roadblocks that are part of being an effective financial professional and have the self-determination, strength, motivation, desire, and conviction it takes to excel.

6. *Money.* We're not talking about being rich. We're talking about being a good money manager. People who are spendthrifts, in debt, in bankruptcy, and who are generally not capable of managing their own finances are not the kind of people who should be advising other people about theirs. The ideal candidate can prove his or her fiscal responsibility and provide six months security while getting started in this business.

7. *Maturity.* Age is not the concern. Leaders don't set age limits. Maturity is another matter. To give financial advice, your people must be mature enough to make intelligent, objective decisions and manage their own lives well enough to help others manage theirs.

With these M&Ms in mind, leaders who *care* about people and carefully *select* their producers will be able to inspire an entire team of producers—each with different goals, different wants, different needs;

some with kids, some without kids; some in debt, some with no debt; those who want fancy stuff, and those who want simple stuff—to do *whatever it takes* to have the life they desire.

When you meet someone who seems to fulfill all these criteria, the Non-Interview is an ideal way to sort the people you wish to formally interview, and it is also a great way to find the wants you can use to motivate that person. What you discover in this conversation can be the tools you'll use later to help a producer become highly successful. As your relationship develops, you will add to your understanding. As a leader, your job will be to help that person reach those goals and achieve those wants.

Whatever they want, you are the leader and coach who will mentor them to achieve it.

For example, in a conversation with Robert you found he has desperately wanted a red Ferrari Testerossa since 1984. You mentally filed it away. Now, when Robert joins your organization, you remember this and work with him to get the Ferrari.

Not every want is a tangible item; some people want stability, others a level of income that will allow a spouse to spend more time with the children, and still others want income that will allow them to put away savings for the future. Whatever they want, you are the leader and coach who will mentor them to achieve it. Their wants becomes something you and they can share and work together to attain.

Because the Non-Interview is an informal event, we've purposefully kept the instructions for doing one as unstructured as possible. As long as you identify the features for which you're looking and follow the general directions, you should now have a useful tool for engaging someone in a conversation to see if there's potential for friendship or business. In the next chapter, we discuss the Values Conversation, which you can use to qualify and select the candidates who will make your organization successful.

CHAPTER **3.**

The Values Conversation:
Laying the Foundation of Trust in Ten Minutes or Less

> People are generally better
> persuaded by the reasons which
> they have themselves discovered
> than by those which have come
> into the mind of others.
>
> BLAISE PASCAL

In 1995, Pete Sampras was fighting a pitched battle against Jim Courier at the Australian Open. Emotions were high as Sampras was down two sets to love when a fan cried out, "C'mon, Pete! Do it for your coach!" That coach was Tim Gullikson, who had recently become seriously ill and couldn't attend the match.

Sampras had a special relationship with his coach, and even the fan may not have known how much that comment would inspire the athlete. So he dug deep, actually shedding tears during the match, and somehow pulled off a historic three-set comeback to win the match.

How many of your producers are moved and inspired by your relationship with them? How many, when the day should be done and it seems they have nothing left inside, dig deep and give it their all one more time for the coach? If you don't have this kind of relationship with the producers who work with you, you might wonder what it would be like if you did. If you do have this kind of relationship, you are among an elite few, and won't it be great to create relationships like this predictably, every time?

Did Sampras give his all because his coach had shown up for the job or because he had helped the young athlete reach the highest ranks of tennis? Beyond that, do you think this relationship was even bigger than the tennis achievements? Which builds bonds in your organization: Finishing your paperwork and making your phone calls, or helping your producers achieve their goals and experience what's most important to them?

To help producers achieve the kind of success they desire, you must learn what they want in their heart of hearts, and they must trust you to care about helping them succeed *for their reasons,* not just for your override. (It's interesting to note that Sampras's fan executed a flawless act of leadership—or was it luck? We don't know. But *you* can do this on purpose.) What would happen to the success of those you lead if you knew exactly what to say to inspire them to dig deep, to perform at their highest level? Can you say the same thing to Mary as to Steve? Is John inspired by the same things as Susan? Of course not. If you can inspire your producers with the same precision as Sampras's fan, you can count on them to execute the plan you developed together for their success. What's more, with trust, you can be completely candid about what it takes to succeed. Do you have the sort of relationship with each of your producers so that when you deliver the perfect nugget of wisdom it's received in a positive way—and acted upon?

The Values Conversation presented in this chapter is a tool for purposefully creating trust and discovering what's important to potential producers in the first five to ten minutes of their first formal interview.* After all, how can your producers believe in your interest in helping them succeed for their reasons if you don't even know what those reasons are? The trust you establish is based on understanding, and there is no better way to truly understand someone than to create a meaningful conversation with them about *their values.* Yet, as with any good conversation,

---

You build trust by listening to their story, not by telling yours.

---

it's not just about the words spoken or the process being followed, but the act of listening and having an intentionally revealing exchange about the character of the other person. With every step of the Values Conversation, the leader implies, "I want to understand what is important to you." You build trust by listening to their story, not by telling yours.

Think of the first interview as like a first date. Would you look across the table at your potential sweetheart and say, "Thank you so much for coming.

---

*If you have read Bill Bachrach's *Values-Based Selling: The Art of Building High-Trust Client Relationships for Financial Advisors, Insurance Agents, and Investment Reps,* you will recognize the Values Conversation. In this book, it has been adapted for creating high-trust *producer* relationships so *leaders* can accomplish two objectives: By conducting the Values Conversation with producers from the outset, you can 1) gain their trust in the first few minutes and 2) demonstrate how you want them to behave with clients. For more information on Values-Based Selling books and tapes, please see the back of this book.

So, let me start the evening off by telling you all about me!" Likewise, when starting a first interview, you wouldn't lead with your background, your track record, how great the company is, etc. Instead, you ask about *them*. The key here is simply to ask what's important to them and then listen, listen, listen. The harder this is for you, the more important it is for you to master.

Trust can and should begin in the first minutes of the recruiting interview (better termed the *selection interview*) and must be nurtured throughout the life of the leader/producer relationship. When you master the Values Conversation, you will be able to understand producers' core values and how to inspire their actions based on their values. Indeed, if your producers are not moved by their own values, there is nothing else you could say or do to inspire them to perform at their highest levels. The Values Conversation will also accomplish these vital objectives:

◆ It will position you as a valuable professional resource, not just another manager trying to get someone—anyone—into the business.

◆ It will quickly flush out time-wasters.

◆ It will build trust and establish an emotional bond.

◆ It will reveal prospective producers' core values, which motivate them to action more effectively than anything else.

◆ It will facilitate accurate goal prioritization.

◆ It will result in a commitment to proceed immediately.

◆ It will improve your relationship with current producers as well as help you understand candidates.

◆ It will enable you to inspire current producers to work with you *without "proselytizing," "seducing," or dangling up-front cash or a bigger payout.*

As you read the sample Values Conversation below, notice how the leader writes the candidate's answers, as they are given, on the stairs starting from the bottom and working to the top.

Leader. We're looking for people who are serious about being successful. My job is to differentiate between the people who say they want to succeed at high levels and the people who are willing to pay the price to do just that. Is success very important to you?

Candidate. Very.

*The values conversation with **producers** always starts with the question: "What's important about success to you?"*

Leader.   **What's important about success *to you?***

Candidate. Making money—enough money to buy the sailboat I want.

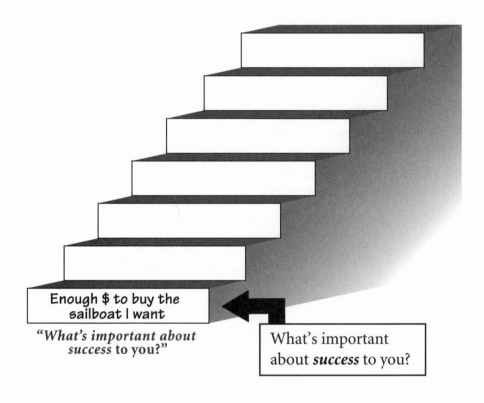

Enough $ to buy the sailboat I want

"What's important about success to you?"

What's important about *success* to you?

Leader. [*After writing "enough $ to buy the sailboat I want" on first step.*] What's important about making enough money, so you can buy the sailboat you want, *to you?*

Candidate. Freedom ... freedom from some things so I have freedom to do others.

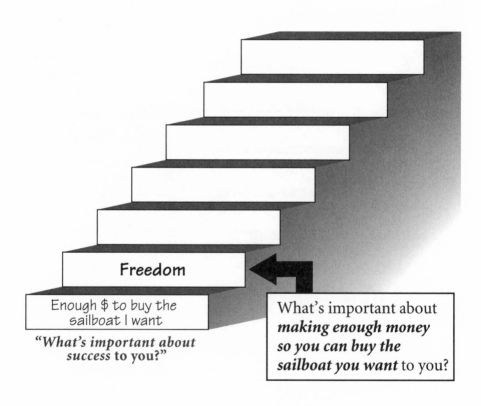

"What's important about *success* to you?"

What's important about *making enough money so you can buy the sailboat you want* to you?

Leader.   When you think about having this freedom, what's important about freedom *to you?*

Candidate.   Time.

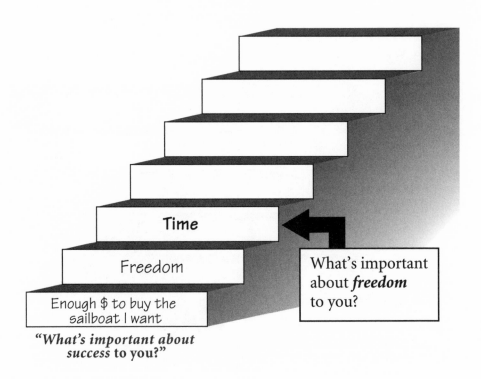

Time

Freedom

Enough $ to buy the sailboat I want

What's important about **freedom** to you?

"What's important about success to you?"

Leader.   So time is very important to you. Help me understand: What's important about time *to you?*

Candidate.   I want time for personal growth, for myself, and for my family as well as for others.

> This is where the emotion begins to escalate substantially. Beyond this point is where the most meaningful responses occur.

Personal Growth for myself and time with my family and others

Time

Freedom

What's important about *time* to you?

Enough $ to buy the sailboat I want

"What's important about success to you?"

Leader. Hmmm. What's important about personal growth and using your time for yourself, your family, and others *to you*?

Candidate. It indicates that I have arrived!

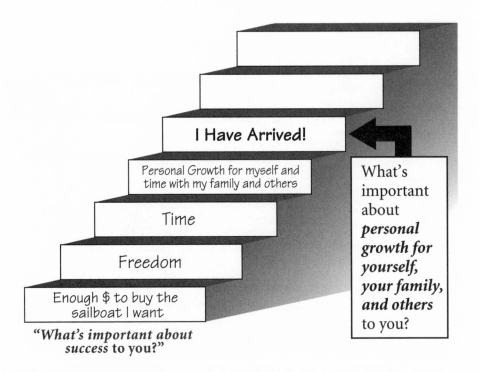

"*What's important about success* **to you?**"

Leader. Wow. It indicates you have arrived.
What's important about the feeling
you have arrived *to you?*

Candidate. Well, it puts me in a position to really
help others and make a difference.

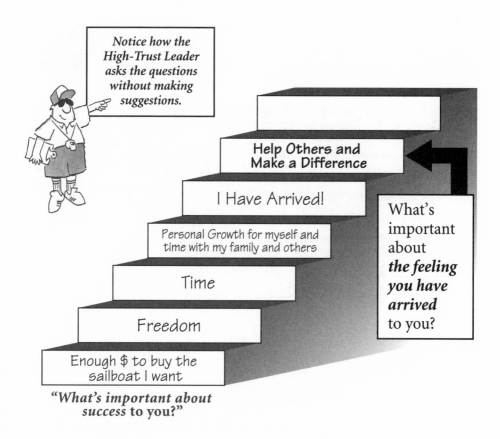

Notice how the
High-Trust Leader
asks the questions
without making
suggestions.

Help Others and
Make a Difference

I Have Arrived!

Personal Growth for myself and
time with my family and others

Time

Freedom

Enough $ to buy the
sailboat I want

What's
important
about
*the feeling
you have
arrived*
to you?

*"What's important about
success to you?"*

Leader.   What's important about helping others and making a difference *to you*?

Candidate.   Then I'll feel like I have truly fulfilled my purpose in life.

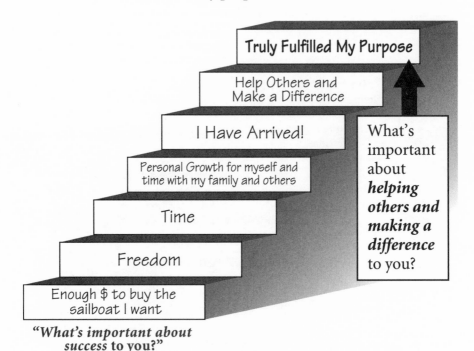

Truly Fulfilled My Purpose

Help Others and Make a Difference

I Have Arrived!

Personal Growth for myself and time with my family and others

Time

Freedom

Enough $ to buy the sailboat I want

What's important about *helping others and making a difference* to you?

"What's important about success to you?"

Leader.   This has been very interesting. I appreciate you sharing all of this with me. Suppose we put together a strategy that would help you be successful enough to have *enough money to buy your sailboat*. More important, you would be able to achieve the *freedom* that will give you the time to have *personal growth for yourself, and time with your family, and others*. Then you can feel like *you have arrived* and you will be in a position to really *help others and make a difference.* Ultimately, you will feel that you have *truly fulfilled your purpose in life.* Is that the kind of career plan you could be committed to?

Candidate. Absolutely!

TIPS FOR AN EFFECTIVE VALUES CONVERSATION

A good relationship between a leader and a producer mirrors a good relationship between a producer and clients. Likewise, your first interview should create the same impression in the minds of prospective producers that you expect them to create with their prospective clients. You need to demonstrate the attitude you want them to have.

1. Listen more than you talk.

2. Remember, this is a conversation, not an interrogation.

3. Go all the way. A common mistake for people new to the Values Conversation is not taking it far enough up the values staircase, where the most meaningful and emotional part of the conversation takes place. The farther you go, the more powerful the bond you will form and the better you will understand your candidate. At the top of the values staircase, you will hear "big picture" values like these:

◆ Fulfilling my purpose in life

◆ Total self-worth

◆ Spiritual fulfillment

◆ Nirvana

◆ Feeling good about myself and my contribution to others

Keep going until you get this kind of answer. Everybody has answers like these, and it's up to you to bring the conversation to this level.

At the risk of sounding redundant, we'll point out that this conversation should be *conversational.* You must be sincerely interested and behave that way. Think of yourself as a facilitator peeling away the layers to the next deeper level of what's important. Discovering and revealing core values is usually a powerful, emotional experience for someone. If you really listen and pay attention as your candidates experience the emotional crescendo of climbing the values staircase, chances are you will have a better understanding of these human beings than almost anyone on the planet—maybe even better than their spouse, and certainly better than any "boss."

The central question—"What's important about success *to you?*"—focuses the conversation on success because, of course, the role of the financial services leader is to help producers become successful in their careers. However, career success is not the ultimate goal. The ultimate goal is to have a great life. *A career is important only to the extent it contributes to a great life.* When your producers believe you care more about their lives than their careers, you will have built a bond of trust. The great news for both of you is

The question, "What's important about success to you?" makes people think.

that a very successful career almost always helps us have an even greater life. Imagine how many successful financial professionals you will attract and develop when you have the skills, the system, and the reputation for helping them generate big production so they can have a great life!

HELP PRODUCERS FULFILL *THEIR* VALUES, NOT YOURS

At least one company in our industry has so bastardized the values-based approach that they actually teach managers to look for people who conform to corporate values rather than helping people fulfill their own values. (We call them managers because real leaders would never do this!) Imagine the outcome: managers who are trying to force company values on producers. How easy it is for the candidate who has learned to interview well to look up those values in an annual report, echo them to the manager, and—bingo!—it's a "fit."

To say that a firm that behaves this way doesn't get it may be the understatement of the century.

The objective is to have a team of producers who all ethically generate large amounts of business. This is far better accomplished by helping producers fulfill their own values than by trying to get them to conform to yours. While this may be painfully obvious to you, we just want you to know that there may be a large number of producers currently working for managers and companies who do not have a clue how to help them fulfill their values. As a leader who knows how to do this, you will attract all the great producers you could ever need or want. By helping them fulfill *their* values, you will achieve *your* goals and fulfill your own values. See how it works?

—BILL BACHRACH

Since we all define a "great life" differently, you must know each of your producers' definitions so you can inspire each of them with their own motives—their own *values,* or what's most important to them. You stay focused on this as you work your way up the values "staircase" by sticking with the format, "What's important about ——————— *to you*?" The conventional sales "wisdom" would be, *Aha! The sailboat is the "hot button."* But read the Values Conversation again and pay special attention to the power of what was said *beyond the sailboat.* The old school manager might have spent fifteen minutes talking about the boat: "What kind? What manufacturer? What size? What kind of finish? New or used? Do you have a boat now? Where will it be moored? How much will it cost? Where do you want to sail it? How long have you been sailing?" No matter how skilled you are at chitchat about sailboats, that discussion pales in comparison to the Values Conversation about making a difference and fulfilling the candidate's purpose in life. Be careful not to get sidetracked by shallow "hot buttons" when it's so easy to slip into the depths of a meaningful human connection. Superficial conversations create superficial relationships. Meaningful connections build high-trust relationships. The most important event that occurs during this interview is that you and the candidate make a meaningful human connection. This is always true and especially important when you are interviewing successful producers who currently work with someone else.

In the Values Conversation, you forego discussion of sailboats and you methodically work your way up the staircase. We've all worked with producers who had lofty goals—then found it a lot easier to change or lower them than to do what was necessary to achieve them. With values, you are dealing with something they can't change or lower. They either do what it takes to fulfill their values or they carry the weight of their dissatisfaction, great or small. Compared to values, the boat sinks. It's the values—the personal, emotional reasons behind the goals—that make the difference. "Freedom," the feeling of having "arrived," the ability to "make a difference," and "fulfill my purpose" will draw this person like a magnet and inspire a producer for a lifetime.

In asking the question "What's important about success *to you*?" and following up to get the highest values as you work your way up the staircase, you create an escalating emotional atmosphere as you demonstrate your interest in the

As you climb the values staircase you will see, feel and hear the nonverbal evidence of escalating emotions.

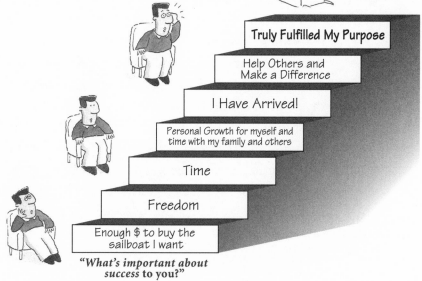

Truly Fulfilled My Purpose

Help Others and Make a Difference

I Have Arrived!

Personal Growth for myself and time with my family and others

Time

Freedom

Enough $ to buy the sailboat I want

"What's important about success to you?"

candidate—not just your interest in selling him or her the career, but your sincere interest in finding out what really matters. With a little practice, you'll use the Values Conversation naturally and be able to put your focus on the candidate, paying attention to voice tone, emotional tenor, confidence, and drive.

Needs, wants, and goals refer to the tangible. Values, on the other hand, are pure, undiluted feelings. Consider the emotional power of values like *freedom, independence, security, pride, providing for family, accomplishment, achievement, balance, making a difference, satisfaction, fulfillment, spiritual attunement, inner peace,* and *self-worth.* These are only a few examples of the values your producers may consider important; you'll find there are many others. Your job is to uncover these values-based emotions so potential producers can see the possibility of a relationship/career working with you in financial services and fulfilling their life values, what is truly and most important to them.

Many people initially miss the true power of the Values Conversation. It's so easy to go only two or three steps up the staircase and think you have it. That's too bad, because it's at the highest level where the greatest connection occurs and the conversation is most meaningful for the other person. This is usually seven to nine answers up the staircase. The most we've experienced is seventeen, and the fewest is three. Regardless of the exact number of "stairs," every complete Values Conversation goes up three "flights," or levels:

Level 1. Easy answers, usually about money, material goods, security, and providing for the family;

Level 2. More thoughtful responses and more abstract answers, such as *freedom, accomplishment, pride, control over my life, time to have more/better experiences, learning and growth, making a difference;* and

Level 3. A significant emotional transition, which could be likened to Abraham Maslow's self-actualization level on his hierarchy of needs. The values now take on an expansive tone: *fulfillment of my destiny or purpose, becoming the best human being I can, spiritual fulfillment, being one with the universe,* and so on.

At the third level, as people share what is most important *to them,* they suddenly see you as much more than a potential boss; they begin to see you as a high-trust leader who cares about them and what's really important to them. They feel honored, respected, and—no doubt—at least a little interested in what else you have to say.

CHAPTER 4.

Five Easy Steps:
Mastering the
Values Conversation

> Never has there been one
> possessed of complete sincerity
> who did not move others.

MENCIUS

Clearly, you don't open an interview by saying, "Hi, I'm Bill. So, uh . . . What's important about success *to you*?" Supporting the simple but meaningful exchange of the Values Conversation are five easy steps—steps every leader must master to conduct it effectively.

1. Set the stage.
2. Reset the stage if necessary.
3. Discover core values using the "What's important about success *to you*?" question and bridging comments.
4. Get precommitment to move forward.
5. Transition into the rest of the interview.

Set the Stage

Setting the stage is the key to positioning yourself as a leader rather than a manager. It's the most effective way to open the Values Conversation, surpassing small talk, chitchat, and talking about yourself, your credentials, your experience, or your company. It paves the way for a smooth Values Conversation, just as the first few minutes of a well-crafted speech earn an audience's attention and positive reaction. Remember, you build trust by listening to their story, not by telling yours.

There are only two rules for setting the stage: Be brief, and end with "What's important about success *to you?*"

Something you gleaned from the Non-Interview or other screening method led you to believe that this person is interested in being even more successful. You can use that information here. Following is an example of setting the stage, which is slightly different from the previous sample dialogue:

Leader. One of the things we do at our firm is hire people who are serious about being successful. We talked about early retirement when we met at the party last week, and this is often one of the benefits of doing very well in this career. Ours is a very rewarding but very challenging business and some people are clearly more serious about success than others. Are you serious about being successful?

Candidate. Absolutely.

Leader. What's important about success
to you?

When you set the stage and ask your candidates what is important about success to them, you are looking for the first answer off the top of their heads— just that first answer, not all the answers. Indeed, there are no right or wrong answers; this is not something candidates can prepare for, nor should you be looking for them to tell you what you want to hear. So set the stage with confidence, and then ask, "What's important about success *to you?*" with genuine interest. Then relax and *listen to the answer.* Proceed at your candidates' pace; you'll learn a lot about their style simply by letting them drive the interview. Remember, this is a conversation, not an interrogation.

The more often you set the stage and use the Values Conversation, the easier the interaction becomes. If you follow the stage-setting formula just as you would a gourmet recipe, the outcome will be equally rewarding. If you take shortcuts or ignore the recipe, you can count on a poor result. The most important thing to remember in setting the stage is never to change the question. Always end with "What's important about success *to you?*"

2 Reset the Stage

Usually, the first time you set the stage you will engage your candidate in the Values Conversation by eliciting the first response. Then you can build on that first response with the subsequent "What's important . . . " questions. However, sometimes candidates don't understand the first question or don't know how to answer. You'll know that's the case if they tell you directly or try to change the subject. An inability to answer may indicate that you need to reset the stage; it can also be an early warning sign that you are dealing with a difficult person. How can you know? You won't be sure until you reset the stage. (Notice it's called *reset the stage* and not *change the question*. If you change the question, you eliminate the effectiveness of the Values Conversation. Never change the question; instead, reset the stage to stay on track.)

If someone responds, "I'm not sure how to answer that," you can empathize. "Yes, I understand," you say, resetting the stage. "It might sound odd at first. Maybe nobody has asked you this before, but please bear with me. It sounds like you and I might make a good team in achieving the level of success you want, so I need to understand what is important about success *to you*. It means different things to different people, and I'm willing to take as much time as you need to understand your perspective. Just off the top of your head, what's important about success *to you*?"

Resetting the stage validates your candidates' feelings without getting off track. If you back off from your predetermined flow of questions (or, worse yet, have no predetermined flow of questions), you will appear weak and unprofessional. If you get nervous and retreat to common ground or other rapport-building tactics, your candidate will wonder what other questions or expectations you are willing to leave unanswered or unfulfilled. Instead of changing course, use a brief stage resetting to explain why you are asking the question. Reassure the candidate that there is no rush or pressure—and that the answer is crucial. Then listen as the candidate answers at his or her own pace. People differ in how long they think before they speak, and you can demonstrate respect with your silence. Never make suggestions to "help" them out. Never put words in their mouth.

Discover Core Values in a Conversational Manner

We all know interviews are question-driven conversations. So the rule is this: If it doesn't end with a question mark, it doesn't belong in the initial interview. The exceptions to the rule are brief statements that set up your next question:

- ◆ *Help me understand.* What's important about ——————— *to you?*

- ◆ *I see.* What's important about ——————— *to you?*

- ◆ *Hmmm. That's interesting.* What's important about ——————— *to you?*

- ◆ ——————— *means different things to different people.* What's important about ——————— *to you?*

We call these statements, which facilitate each question of the Values Conversation and make it flow, "bridging comments." You can use bridging comments to avoid sounding like an interrogator. Listen and go at the candidate's pace.

Get Precommitment

Precommitment begins to establish the basic ground rules of the producer-leader relationship. It provides evidence that candidates are serious about their success. Precommitment affirms the idea that you and the prospective producers are establishing a professional *relationship* to help them fulfill their values. Precommitment is not about trapping candidates into making a decision right now; it's about establishing the rules of the relationship and conveying that you understand what's important to them. Here's a review of the precommitment you read earlier.

Leader.   This has been very interesting. I appreciate you sharing all of this with me. Suppose we put together a strategy that would help you be successful enough to have the money to buy your sailboat. More important, you would be able to achieve the freedom that will give you the time to have personal growth and allow you to do things for yourself, your family, and others. Then you can feel like you have arrived and you will be in a position to really help others and make a difference. Ultimately, you will feel that you have truly fulfilled your purpose in life. Is that the kind of career plan you could be committed to?

Candidate. Absolutely!

Leader. How hard would you be willing to work to make that a reality?

Candidate. Whatever it takes.

Understanding your candidates' values early in the conversation causes the momentum to shift so they want to embark on this career more than you want to start them in the business. Just as it makes more sense for a producer to use a client's buying momentum than to apply selling pressure, it makes more sense for you to use your candidates' hunger for success instead of trying to sell them on the business. This isn't just a positioning tactic; the simple truth is that if they don't want what's important to them more than you want it for them, this relationship isn't going to work. The shift from passive interview to active pursuit of the job occurs when candidates discover their emotional reasons (their values) for wanting success. The connection between core values and success creates professional momentum.

If the answer to your precommitment question is yes, you have established an agreement in principle between you and your candidate.

Transition into an In-Depth Interview

If you've gotten this far, you've established that both parties are interested, but no commitment has been made. For both of you to make a final decision about working together or not, you must engage in an in-depth interview. You may transition into their goals and their drive to achieve them. The transition would sound something like this:

> **Leader.** Now that I understand what's important to you and I think I have more of a sense of who you are, we should talk about your tangible goals as well as help you get some perspective about where you stand right now. Where would you like to start?

> **Candidate.** Let's talk about my goals.

It is now appropriate to have a detailed discussion about the sailboat or any other tangible goal (such as retirement, sending children to college, what kind of home and car they want to own, what kind of vacations they like to take, etc.) that may have come up either during this interview or previously during the Non-Interview.

The big difference between values and goals is that you can attach a price tag to a goal, but values are about pure emotion. The Values Conversation gives you an intimate understanding of candidates' emotional motives—motives that can solidify their drive to achieve success in your business. During the in-depth interview, you gain valuable information about the gap that exists between where they are today and where they want to be. This is the foundation of the visual representation of a producer's career path, the professional Success Road Map discussed in Chapter 5. This road map makes the current reality and the desired future as clear as possible, emphasizing the values the producer will experience along the way.

There are no absolutes in determining whether or not candidates will be successful based on their values, but you can definitely get some clues. Some are tangible, and some are found through intuition. The key issues in this first selection interview are whether or not the potential producer is coachable and if they have the commitment to put that coaching into consistent action.

It's not about potential. You only have to look to sports to find apt analogies for the great talent with huge potential who is just not coachable, won't play by the rules, or won't work within the system. This is one of the challenges leaders face. They invest in potential and see what a person is capable of, but the reality is that the leader must have systems in place that are proven to help producers succeed, and they have to hire people who are willing to follow and execute those systems. Both sides of the equation are crucial. Part of your job is to keep people focused on why (the emotional reason) they are doing what is required to succeed in a financial services career. Understanding their values will help you present a career plan in their terms, their values, and for their emotional reasons—and consistently hold them to it.

Although there are managers who talk a good game but don't actually have a system to help producers, by and large it's the other way around. Do you ever find yourself caring more about your producers' success than they do? That's why being selective is so important. The leader must have complete confidence in the system's ability to work for the producers; by the same token, he or she must have complete confidence in the producer's ability and willingness to work the system.

Engaging prospective producers in the Values Conversation teaches you to focus on the emotion behind the answers more than the responses themselves. Can you feel how badly they want it? Is there fire in their eyes? When you challenge their level of commitment to do what it takes, do they respond

The better they are, the better you have to be to attract them.

calmly or is there an emotional "I'll show you!" reaction? The people who are truly committed to fulfilling their values have an intensity when they discuss what is important to them. And those with intensity can spot your sincerity or lack of it a mile away. The Values Conversation is an invaluable tool, but if you don't really care about your candidates, it will not work. When you do care, either you quickly establish high-trust relationships with producers who will take action on the training you provide, or you quickly dismiss those who would have wasted your time or become difficult un-producers.

In some cases, it takes only one meeting to make a decision—a candidate looks hot, seems ready to go, is on fire and coachable. All of that is evident in the rare individual, and you may decide to make an offer during the initial meeting. On the other hand, there will be many candidates you view positively, but you need more meetings to become convinced—or they may need more meetings to become convinced you are the leader they want to follow. The better they are, the better you have to be to attract them.

Once you have built a values staircase and know what's important to them, look for evidence in their lives that is consistent with their values. We all know producers who look like a million dollars and talk a great game, but never amount to anything. Don't rely on their values alone; get evidence. As you introduce the Values Conversation into your selection interview, certain patterns should emerge to help you make choices about who to hire and who to avoid. Candidates who trust you and have a burning desire to fulfill their values are far more likely to succeed.

CHAPTER 5.

The Success Road Map:
Inspiring Producers to Succeed for Their Own Reasons

> The vital, successful people
> I have met all had one
> common characteristic.
> They had a plan.
>
> MARILYN VAN DERBUR

Imagine you are on an airplane. You are calmed by the pilot's voice over the loudspeaker, which conveys confidence and experience. You relax into your seat and trust the ability of the pilot to get you to your destination. However, your feelings quickly change during takeoff. As the plane falters, you get that queasy feeling in the pit of your stomach and think, *Oh, boy. This pilot sounded good, but maybe there's no competence here.* Do producers ever feel that way about your piloting abilities?

A frequent comment we hear from producers is that managers promise more than they deliver. There's no doubt conducting a brilliant interview that builds trust sets you up for success. But then you do have to deliver. You begin as the relationship starts to take off, as you outline the benefits of a career with you. As a highly trusted leader, you are expected to support, coach, and guide producers, and there's no time like the present to show a candidate that when you say you'll do something, you mean it.

The obvious next step after you have had a Values Conversation and discussed goals with someone is to talk about how you can help him or her experience those values and achieve those goals through a position with your company. You can do this with any number of tools. The two we will offer you in this chapter are the Career Rater and the professional Success Road Map. Both can be used with all types of candidates.

The Career Rater piques candidates' interest as they complete a simple form. This document asks candidates to compare their current work environment against an ideal work environment, causing them to seriously consider what level of satisfaction is gained by their current position or profession. (See pages 71–72 for an illustration of the Career Rater.) Candidates would fill out the first half of this survey "blind" (without seeing the other half), so they could objectively evaluate satisfaction with the various aspects of a current job or profession. When that is complete, you present the second half, which asks the candidates to speculate about the satisfaction level in an ideal work environment. This not only gives you clues about what is important to them in a work context, but also makes candidates more aware of their satisfaction or dissatisfaction with their current career.

The comprehensive Success Road Map shown on pages 74–75 has a similar goal. You can see that it visually represents the road leading from the "current reality" to meeting goals and experiencing values along the way. It shows how working with you will bridge the gap between the current reality and the desired future. It is designed to provide the following.

PLEASE RATE THE FOLLOWING
AS THEY RELATE TO YOUR
PRESENT CAREER

(1 = LOW   2 = MODERATE   3 = GOOD   4 = HIGH   5 = EXCELLENT)

1. Success record of organization	1	2	3	4	5
2. Prestige and recognition	1	2	3	4	5
3. Challenge	1	2	3	4	5
4. Professional status	1	2	3	4	5
5. Decision-making opportunities	1	2	3	4	5
6. Management concern for your business	1	2	3	4	5
7. Chance for management	1	2	3	4	5
8. Chance for part of complete ownership	1	2	3	4	5
9. Ability to control your own time	1	2	3	4	5
10. Ability to control your own earnings	1	2	3	4	5
11. Chance for high earnings ($100,000+)	1	2	3	4	5
12. Choice of people you associate with	1	2	3	4	5
13. Regular contact with the public	1	2	3	4	5
14. Worthy service to public	1	2	3	4	5
15. Retirement and fringe benefits	1	2	3	4	5

PLEASE RATE THE FOLLOWING
AS THEY WOULD RELATE TO YOUR
IDEAL CAREER

(1 = LOW   2 = MODERATE   3 = GOOD   4 = HIGH   5 = EXCELLENT)

1.	Success record of organization	1	2	3	4	5
2.	Prestige and recognition	1	2	3	4	5
3.	Challenge	1	2	3	4	5
4.	Professional status	1	2	3	4	5
5.	Decision-making opportunities	1	2	3	4	5
6.	Management concern for your business	1	2	3	4	5
7.	Chance for management	1	2	3	4	5
8.	Chance for part of complete ownership	1	2	3	4	5
9.	Ability to control your own time	1	2	3	4	5
10.	Ability to control your own earnings	1	2	3	4	5
11.	Chance for high earnings ($100,000+)	1	2	3	4	5
12.	Choice of people you associate with	1	2	3	4	5
13.	Regular contact with the public	1	2	3	4	5
14.	Worthy service to public	1	2	3	4	5
15.	Retirement and fringe benefits	1	2	3	4	5

The essence of the professional Success Road Map is to demonstrate how your system helps producers bridge the gap between where they are now and where they want to be so they can enjoy the tangible payoff of reaching their goals and the emotional payoff of experiencing their values.

◆ A one-page inspirational look at the candidate's future

◆ A simple perspective from which choices can be made easily

◆ A useful tool from which a high-trust relationship can be established

◆ A comprehensive source of information so an effective action plan can be created

◆ A vehicle for the high-trust leader and producer to discover exactly what has to be done to move the producer's business to the next level of success

◆ A snapshot that makes it easy to identify the resources that will propel a producer to his or her highest level of success

Success Road Map

"There are those who travel and those
who are going somewhere.
They are different, and yet they are the same.
Successful people have this over their rivals:
they know where they are going."

Mark Caine

CATEGORY	NOW	WANT TO BE
___	___	___
___	___	___
___	___	___
___	___	___
___	___	___
___	___	___
___	___	___
___	___	___
___	___	___
___	___	___
___	___	___

"What's Important About Success to You?"

(continue as needed)

Personal Goals "Milestones"

Personal Goals "Milestones"

Personal Goals "Milestones"

To incorporate the Success Road Map into your interviewing process, simply start using it during the Values Conversation and goals discussion by writing the values on the staircase and the goals in the milestone boxes provided. (If there aren't enough boxes, you can draw more.) The goals conversation can cover all aspects of your producers' life. What kind of goals might you encounter? Your producers have the same goals as their clients: financial independence; sending their kids or grandchildren to college; buying a home, car, vacation home, and country club membership; taking annual vacations or attending special, once-in-a-lifetime trips or events; taking care of an elderly loved one, etc.

Is this really the manager's job? Absolutely— well, the high-trust leader thinks so, especially concerning the issue of financial independence. A leader can't imagine anything worse than a team of producers, claiming to be financial professionals capable of helping clients make smart financial choices, whose own financial lives are in complete chaos. The typical sales manager doesn't care about the producers' personal financial situation as long as production is good; in contrast, *the high-trust leader cares as much about the producer's life as about production.* Most leaders would rather get out of the business than live and work with producers who are so lacking in integrity.

The difference between what high-trust leaders do for their producers and what producers do for their clients is that the leader helps producers earn income *and* handle it properly so they can achieve their goals.

The producer probably does not influence clients' incomes, and solely helps them with the plan and the implementation.

Completing the Success Road Map with a candidate means having a thorough conversation about goals, which contains three basic components, once the goal is identified:

1. a specific amount of money to be made,

2. a specific date this goal is to be realized, and

3. an emotionally compelling reason for reaching the goal.

Each of these components has a corresponding question which will yield the proper information. Let's say the first goal is to achieve financial independence.

1. Amount of money: "How much money— net, spendable—will you want per month at the point in your life when work has become optional?" You are looking for an amount of money to be spent, not the amount of assets they need to create that income (a figure like $15,000 per month). It is your job to calculate how big the pool of assets needs to be to generate that income.

2. Date: "By what date in the future do you want to be in this position?" You are looking for a specific date, not a year or a number of years from now (an answer like April 23, 2019).

3. Emotionally Compelling Reason: "Let's imagine the date is April 23, 2019 and you know you have enough assets to generate $15,000 of income every month for the rest of your life whether you continue to work or not. Give me three words that describe what you are thinking and feeling now that you are in this position." Look for superlatives that trigger powerful, compelling emotions.

Here's how it sounds in conversation.

Leader.   Now that I know what's important to you, the next thing I need to know is what your goals are. I am especially interested in the long-term goals that will require some money and planning to achieve. What's the first goal that comes to mind for you?

Candidate.   Someday I'd like to be able to retire, or at least be in a position to stop working whenever I want.

Leader.   Very good. I think that's especially important because it makes sense for people who are giving others advice about becoming financially independent to be on that same path themselves. You probably have an idea of what kind of lifestyle you would like to have when work becomes optional. How much net, spendable money do you need or want to have to pay for this lifestyle?

Candidate.   Do you mean after taxes, the net amount that I need to pay my bills plus how much I need to pay for all the things I want to do when I'm retired?

Leader. Exactly.

Candidate. Are we talking today's dollars or should I factor in inflation?

Leader. Today's dollars. I'll factor in inflation when I work out the numbers.

Candidate. I think that would require fifteen thousand dollars per month.

Leader. Okay. Now let's pick a date when you are going to be in a position to make that a reality. Remember, you don't actually have to retire. We're just talking about setting a target when work becomes optional for you. By what date would you like to be in this financial position?

Candidate. Well, I guess fifteen to twenty years from now.

Leader. We need to be more specific than that. We need to pick a specific year, month, and day.

Candidate. Wow, you're serious?

Leader. You bet I am. My role is to help you hit your target and it's hard to hit a target that's not specific. Just like you have to help your clients plan for and hit specific targets, I have to do the same for you.

Candidate. Okay. How about April 23, 2019.

> **Leader.** That's great. Can you tell me what's special about that day?
>
> **Candidate.** That's my birthday, and I think work becoming optional would be a great present to myself!
>
> **Leader.** I think so, too. Let's take a walk into the future: It's now your birthday, April 23, in the year 2019, and you've done it. You have made a great living, you have saved and invested well, and you are now in a position where work is optional. What are two or three words that describe what you are thinking and how you are feeling now that you are in this position?
>
> **Candidate.** Yahoo! I've arrived. I've made it. I accomplished for myself what I have been helping my clients achieve. Relief!
>
> **Leader.** That's terrific. I will be really happy for you and your family when we celebrate your accomplishment.

You will notice how easy it is to get people to come up with a date when you ask. It will frequently be January 1, December 31, or a special day like a birthday or an anniversary. The more specific the target, the more realistic and believable the goal.

As a high-trust leader, you will have this specific conversation about every short- and long-term goal your producer has. Most of these goals will require money to achieve, either directly or indirectly. "Directly" means the goal costs money, such as buying a vacation home. "Indirectly" means the producer needs to set aside enough money to have the freedom to take the time off for something like a sabbatical, religious mission work, or training for the Hawaii Ironman Triathlon.

You are probably thinking that having these conversations and building a Success Road Map would be a really good thing to do with all of your existing producers and not just candidates. You are right. It is especially important that you do so before someone else does.

After concluding your discussion of the candidate's or producer's goals, you can make a natural transition into a conversation about the current reality represented by the box on the lower left of the Success Road Map. Here you can make notes about a number of factors in the person's current reality.

The current reality section will require some finesse as well as continued attention to the candidate. You must determine which topics are appropriate to broach and which are irrelevant. Following is a list of possible items, representing what we would generally cover in an interview. These topics can be represented in the "category/now/want to be" section as a description of the kind of career and the kind of professional this person wants to build and become. Take a look at the example on pages 96–98 to see how this can be done.

Money:

- gross income (either for the person or for a business if the candidate is an owner)
- personal income
- net worth

If the candidate is already a producer, break the income into categories, such as fees for planning, fees for assets under management, and commissions.

Time:

- time off in the last twelve months
- days worked in a week
- average number of hours worked in a day
- use for additional time off

The following are for candidates already in a sales- or production-oriented profession (Some apply only if the candidate is in financial services now.)

Referrals:

- percent of appointments that originate from a referral

Assets under management:

- mutual funds
- managed money
- cash-value life insurance
- annuities
- other

Business expenses for marketing:

- mailers
- seminars
- cold callers
- other

The following demonstration is a sample conversation between a leader and a candidate currently successful in financial services, utilizing the topics listed above.*

Leader. Now that we have had a thorough discussion about what's important to you and your goals, we should take a look at your current reality. I know you are already a successful producer. My experience is that it is usually the successful producers who tend to seek even higher levels of success. Do you believe that you have an higher level of success than you have already achieved?

Producer. Absolutely.

Leader. I thought so. While there are many ways to measure success in our business, there are a few common denominators. I am going to ask you some very specific questions about where you are now and where you want to be with regard to some of these success measures. I can assure you that everything we discuss is confidential. Okay?

Producer. Sure.

---

*We recognize that various branches of the financial services industry view recruiting from other firms differently. Many people in the insurance industry consider this unethical, while many others in the insurance and securities industries consider this commonplace. As such, this dialogue can be viewed either as a proactive recruiting example, or as an example of what might happen if producers were to approach the high-trust leader on their own. It can also be loosely viewed as an outline of the kind of conversation a high-trust leader would have with his or her own producers in helping them move to a higher level within the organization.

Leader.	The first area worth discussing is money. We are in the money business, so it makes sense that one way we measure our own success is by money. How much is your current gross production?
Producer.	Well, it's a combination of securities commissions, insurance commissions, and fee income. The total is three hundred eighty five thousand dollars.
Leader.	Where would you like your gross production to be?
Producer.	Next year I'd like to do five hundred thousand, and ultimately I'd really like to be at one million.
Leader.	That's a great goal. Maybe we'll be able to make that happen. After your split with your firm and your business expenses, how much is left for your personal income?
Producer.	Before taxes?
Leader.	Yes, your gross personal income.
Producer.	About a hundred and fifty thousand.
Leader.	And where would you really like your personal income to be?
Producer.	If I could have a personal income of two hundred fifty to five hundred thousand, I'd be golden.

Leader.	Very good. One of the things we strive to do is to help our producers achieve financial independence. I know this is important for you because we talked about it. What is your current net worth?
Producer.	Not including my home equity, my cars, and stuff like that, we have accumulated about four hundred thousand dollars toward being financially independent.
Leader.	Congratulations; you're well on your way.

Let's pause this conversation for a moment. You may be wondering why a candidate you hardly know would talk about all of this personal information with you. In a word, it's—you guessed it—*trust*. That trust has been built from how sincerely you *listened* during the Non-Interview and Values Conversation. These are both credibility-building human interactions. Use them effectively, and your candidates will be anxious to provide you with any and all information that will help you help them.

If you have extensive training or experience in high-pressure sales, you may tend to view the world through a lens of being distrusted. So it may be hard to imagine what it will be like when people trust you implicitly, answer your questions with total candor, and do whatever you tell them to do. If people are not opening up to you, it's probably because they feel as if they are being recruited—that you want something from them more than you truly want to help them. If you continue to behave like a "push" salesperson, whether you're peddling a financial services product or career, you will continue to live in a world where you are not trusted. If you change your behavior to the ways of the "pull" high-trust leader, however, you can live in a world where people trust you and follow you.

Back to our conversation:

Leader.   Let's shift gears away from the money and discuss quality of life. I know you love your work, but quality of life is really about having the time to do other things that matter to you. How much time off, real vacation time—not company conferences—have you taken in the last year?

Producer.   Take out the company trip and I took two weeks vacation.

Leader.   How much time off would you like to be taking?

Producer.   At least four weeks every year.

Leader..   Yes, that sounds better. At our firm, we're really big on being very productive, but doing it in a way that you get to have a great quality of life. Let's talk about your work week. How many days per week do you work?

Producer.   I used to work five days a week and most of Saturday. Now I work five

days and just a few hours on the
weekend to catch up on paperwork.

Leader.   Does that mean five and a half?

Producer.   That's about right.

"At our firm, we're really big on being very productive, but doing it in a way that you get to have a great quality of life."

Leader.   How many hours per day do you
work?

Producer.   The days are still pretty long. I'd say a
good ten hours.

Leader.   How many days and hours would you
like to work?

Producer.   As long as I could keep the production
up I'd be thrilled to work four days a
week!

Leader.   Sounds great to me. You know there
are people in our business who do a
million or more of production and
have four-day work weeks.

Producer.   I've heard that; I just haven't figured
out how yet.

Leader.   Tell me a few things you would do
with your time if you had two more
weeks of vacation every year and only
worked four days per week.

Producer. Oh, boy! That's easy. First I'd play one more round of golf every week. I'd spend more quality time with my family every week. It's very clear to me that I won't be able to make up that time with them later. I'd like to read more books that are not work-related. When I was in college I was in much better physical condition, and I'd love to get back in shape. We live in a great state and there are dozens of one- and two-day getaways that my spouse and I would love to experience, with and without the kids. As far as vacations, we'd take one more ski trip with the whole family, and we've always wanted to visit Ireland. I could go on for hours. Trust me—we will not have a hard time figuring out what to do with more free time.

Leader. Yes, it sounds like there is much you could do that would enhance your quality of life. Ultimately, the best way to add the kinds of clients you want is by referral. When you meet with a prospect whom you have never met before, what percentage of these first interviews come from a referral?

Producer. That really hits me where I live. I'll bet not more than twenty percent of my new clients come from referrals. I think I do a great job for my clients, but for some reason I don't get a lot of unsolicited referrals and I haven't gotten comfortable asking on a regular basis. I know I should, but I end up doing the same old prospecting and marketing things I've always done.

Leader. Well, you're not alone. Very few producers seem to master referrals. But we can work on it. Most of the producers we work with have certain clients who are better than others. These clients are usually selected by a combination of how much money they have and if their personality makes them especially enjoyable to work with. We call them Ideal Clients. What's your definition of an Ideal Client?

Producer. I never thought about that, but it's true—some clients are much more profitable and fun to work with than others. I probably haven't defined this as clearly as I could, but I'd say I work best with small business owners who are very happily married, have a few kids, are so busy running their business that they prefer to delegate their financial decisions to me and follow my advice without much hassle, and have personal incomes of two hundred thousand plus. I also really like working with retired business owners who have a bunch of money but don't like messing with it because they are too busy living the good life.

Leader. That's a pretty good definition. How many of these Ideal Clients do you have now?

Producer. Not enough. Probably twenty-five or thirty at the most.

Leader. What would your life be like if you had fifty by the end of this year?

Producer. It would be incredible! Much more profitable. Much more time-effective.

Leader. It sure would. One of the more important things for us to keep track of in this business is assets under management. I understand that you may have to guesstimate the answers to these questions, but do the best you can for me. What do you think is the value of your total assets under management?

Producer. I think I know this pretty accurately. About thirty-five million.

Leader. Can you break it down between managed accounts, mutual funds, cash value life insurance, annuities, and any other type of business you do?

Producer.   I can try. Most of it is in mutual funds, probably twenty million. Then about five million each in managed accounts, variable life, and fixed and variable annuities.

Leader.   How much in assets under management would you like to have?

Producer.   I always thought one hundred million sounded really good.

"The reason I have been asking these questions is so I can get to know you better. I also want to get a sense of how serious you are about taking your business to the next level."

Leader.   That does have a nice ring to it. How much money would you estimate you spend every month on expenses for prospecting and marketing, direct mail, cold-callers, advertising, seminars, etc.?

Producer.   It varies depending on the month, but I probably spend an average of about five thousand.

Leader.   How much would you like to spend on prospecting and marketing?

Producer.   Well zero would be nice, but I don't think that's realistic.

Leader.   I understand. The reason I have been asking these questions is so I can get to know you better. I also want to get a sense of how serious you are about taking your business to the next level. You've worked at your current firm for a long time, so you know exactly the support you get or don't get to make your business really successful there. Based on that experience and your experience with me so far, where do you think you would get the better support to take your business to the next level?

Producer.   Well, frankly, you understand more about me personally and my business after an hour than my manager knows about me after eight years. I'm still interested in finding out more about exactly what you do, but my gut reaction is you could probably help me take my business to the next level better than where I am now.

     The power of the tools and methods in this book is that they support you in pursuing a relationship instead of forcing an outcome. You can be genuinely interested in people, and if there's a fit, great. If not, you can truly enjoy getting to know the other person and not feel compelled to force anything. If you approach recruiting in this way, it's fun and interesting. The right people will be attracted, and the wrong people will not. Nobody is sold. Lots of people will "buy," but they will never feel sold.

Once you and the candidate are looking at the completed Success Road Map, you will find out if he or she is sincerely interested in moving forward. There's no need for pressure. If so, now or at the next interview, you can propose an expanded action plan for making this map a reality. The motives are obvious, and the path is clear. The choice will be obvious. As you'll learn in the next few chapters, this plan will include

- ◆ action items and a "behavior checklist" to be successful;
- ◆ training: some in advance and some as you go;
- ◆ introduction to your array of resources, such as outside training and internal resources;
- ◆ what the relationship will be like if the new producer implements, and what it will be like if he or she does not;
- ◆ clear standards of production and behavior with predetermined consequences and benefits; and
- ◆ a reality check about what it will take to succeed.

The risk, of course, is that a producer will take your plan and implement it with someone else. That's possible, but have faith in the human connection. You will have done more for this person than anyone they have ever met in the business. The Success Road Map creates tremendous clarity and inspiration. The action plan contains a few golden eggs, but you are the goose who lays them. If you have truly connected and you are dealing with a reasonably intelligent human being, your candidate will recognize the value of getting your golden eggs on an ongoing basis, plus the benefit of implementation support. If not, writing an action plan is a small price to pay to discover a candidate's true nature.

You can propose the action plan much in the way a producer would propose the writing of a comprehensive financial plan:

Leader. Based on what we've discussed and written on your Success Road Map, I could create for you a basic action plan for what I think would be required for you to take your business to the next level. I don't mind investing some time to do that for you, but I need to get a sense of where you stand, because I'm not in the action-plan-writing business. Let's say that I create a viable action plan for you, and you believe that my firm has the capacity to help you implement it. On a scale from one to ten, how likely would you be to come to work with us?

Producer. I'd say at least a seven or eight.

Leader. Would you like me to create that basic action plan for you?

Producer. Yes.

Leader.   When would you like to get together
             to go over it?

By designing and presenting a Success Road
Map for your candidates or existing producers, you
demonstrate a powerful tool they can not only use to
keep their own careers on track, but a method they can
also implement with clients. You have put yourself in a
position to teach them how to use the Non-Interview
and Values Conversation with clients (they simply
change the question to "What's important about
money *to you*?") and to construct a Financial Road
Map (a client's version of the Success Road Map) for
them. You are fulfilling the high-trust leader's first
duty: to teach by example.

Presenting the Success Road Map

The most valuable service you can provide to
candidates is to act as a guide, helping them create the
life they want. Like a travel agent helping a customer
plan a trip around the world, the high-trust leader has
an important task to accomplish. You need to stay
focused on explaining the plan for your producers'
professional journey.

Success Road Map

"There are those who travel and those
who are going somewhere.
They are different, and yet they are the same.
Successful people have this over their rivals:
they know where they are going."
   Mark Caine

CATEGORY	NOW	WANT TO BE
Gross Production	$285,000	$500,000
Personal Income	$100,000	$250,000 within 2 yrs. ultimately $500K
Net Worth	$600,000	$3,000,000
Debt	$250,000	Zero
Cash Reserves	$20,000	$40,000
Time Off	2 weeks	6 weeks
Work Week	5-1/2 days/ 55 hours	4 days/ 32 hours
Ideal Clients	25	50
Referrals	10% of First Interviews	100%
Assets Under Management	25 million	100 million
Life Insurance in Force	25 million	100 million
No. of Financial Plans Written to Date	46	100 by year-end
No. of Effective Staff People	1	3

"What's Important About Success to You?"

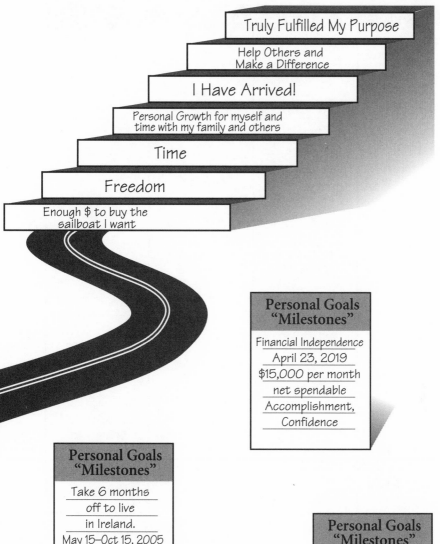

Truly Fulfilled My Purpose

Help Others and
Make a Difference

I Have Arrived!

Personal Growth for myself and
time with my family and others

Time

Freedom

Enough $ to buy the
sailboat I want

**Personal Goals
"Milestones"**

Financial Independence
April 23, 2019
$15,000 per month
net spendable
Accomplishment,
Confidence

**Personal Goals
"Milestones"**

Take 6 months
off to live
in Ireland.
May 15–Oct 15, 2005
$35,000
In Control, Happy

**Personal Goals
"Milestones"**

Buy new home:
at least 2,500
sq. ft. on 3 acres
July 1, 2009
$350,000 purchase price
$50,000 cash needed
Relaxed, Comfortable

*To receive a free sample of a blank Success
Road Map, fax your address and request to
Bachrach & Associates, Inc. at (619) 558-0748,
or e-mail us at info@bachrachvbs.com.*

Benchmarking Success

Category	Where I Am Now	I Want to Be	Notes
Gross Production	$285,000	$500,000	
Personal Income	$100,000	$250,000 within 2 yrs.	ultimately $500,000
Net Worth	$600,000	$3,000,000	
Debt	$250,000	Zero	
Cash Reserves	$20,000	$40,000	
Time Off	2 weeks	6 weeks	
Work Week	5-$\frac{1}{2}$ days/ 55 hours	4 days/ 32 hours	
Ideal Clients	25	50	
Referrals	10% of First Interviews	100%	
Assets Under Management	25 million	100 million	
Life Insurance in Force	25 million	100 million	
No. of Financial Plans Written to Date	46	100 by year-end	eventually 200
No. of Effective Staff People	1	3	

The purpose of this chart is to benchmark a candidate's current level of success so you can create a specific, step-by-step action plan for bridging the gap between where they are now and where they want to be and, ultimately, so they achieve their goals and enjoy more of what's important to them.

Because high-trust leaders are at least as concerned with the person as the production, they don't beat people over the head about their shortcomings or weaknesses. The high-trust leader inspires people to reach for the next level while offering to help them make it happen. Who would you rather have as a leader: someone who focuses on your weaknesses or someone who inspires you to fulfill your greatness?

Using a visual aid like the sample we've provided on pages 96–97, recap your potential producer's values, goals, and current reality. Effective representation of the gap between the current situation and the personal milestones—which leads to the ultimate fulfillment of what is important to you—elicits an emotional response that is the most powerful way to begin this part of the meeting. Use the Success Road Map to graphically represent your potential producer's professional portrait.

> **Leader.** Earlier, you told me it is important for you to be successful so you can ——————— [*naming the values and pointing to the Success Road Map*]. You also have shared your specific goals with me.
>
> As you can see, there is a gap between where you are now and where you want to be. My job, if we decide to go to work together, is to help you bridge that gap not only so you can achieve these goals, but also, ultimately, so you can enjoy the feeling of fulfilling what is important to you. I have come up with a strategy designed specifically to do that for you. Are you ready to review it?

Once the career opportunity has been presented both visually and in terms candidates can relate to (a Success Road Map plus a detailed action plan), they can make a decision, perhaps on the spot, perhaps after some thought, perhaps after the next meeting where a spouse may be present. It's also possible that a candidate will say he or she wants to think it over and then never return your calls. *There is no wrong decision.* When candidates choose to participate, they've made the right choice. When candidates choose not to participate, they've made the right choice. The harder you have to sell the candidate on the job, the harder you will probably have to work to get that person to implement the career strategy you formulate. (Do you have any producers who, if you knew then what you know now, you never would have taken on?) The more comfortable and natural the fit, the more likely you are to have continually self-motivated producers who are more committed to their success than you are. Keep in mind that it's not unusual for people to go out and check with other financial services organizations to compare the level of support and financial opportunities they offer. Yet if you've done a good job in building a high-trust interpersonal relationship, that will overcome any so-called competition.

The bottom line? "Walking your talk" from the very beginning with candidates: really *listening* during the Non-Interview and Values Conversation, and developing a Success Road Map you know they will be inspired to follow. We already mentioned that producers frequently discuss how their managers were a lot better at convincing them to come on board ("selling the job") than they are at helping them build a successful career. Meanwhile, many managers lament how producers seem unwilling to do what it takes to succeed. Who is right? Perhaps both, but it's *your* job to inspire producers to learn from you and use what they learn to achieve what they've set out to accomplish. Your guidance, experience, and friendship are all crucial assets to producers, whether they know it or not. It's up to you to ensure they know it.

6.

The Groundwork of Greatness:
Developing Relationships to
Move Producers to the Next Level

> Every time you see a turtle
> atop a fence post,
> you know it had some help.
>
> ANONYMOUS

McDonald's, the world's largest and most successful fast-food franchise, is everywhere. Every nook and cranny of every city, town, and burg in America is lit up by the Golden Arches. In fact, the company spends millions of dollars each year on site planning and employs a score of people whose job it is to research each potential location. McDonald's uses a formula that takes into consideration many variants: size of the area, growth patterns, tax rates, traffic count, neighboring commercial success rate, etc. Out of all this compiled information they pick locations and build brand-spanking-new red and yellow structures complete with towering arches.

Burger King also has a site planning team. Their formula for deciding where to build a restaurant is much simpler: They wait for McDonald's to announce their newest location, then go out and buy land across the street.

Which is right? They both are. Certainly no one will argue with the success of a strategy with "over billions and billions served." Though not as complex, Burger King's model works just as well and saves hundreds of thousands of dollars. The two successful companies have one thing in common: They both have systems that work.

Your success as a leader in the financial services industry requires the same—a system for helping your producers reach their goals, no matter how lofty they may be.

Climbing Mount Everest is a daunting challenge for even the most seasoned mountaineer. Reaching the top, or "summiting" the 29,000-foot peak is achieved by only a fraction of those who attempt the climb. One of the most important factors contributing to the success of any expedition to the tallest mountain in the world is the base camp. It's a site around 18,000 feet equipped with tents, oxygen, warm clothes, food, and medical staff and supplies. Base camp is the starting and fall-back point for those going up. In case of emergency—violent storms, injury, altitude sickness—climbers can always go back down to base camp. It's where anyone, regardless of sex, age, or climbing ability, begins the ascent. Climbers feel safe there because they are provided the tools, both physical and emotional, they need to make it to the next camp and beyond.

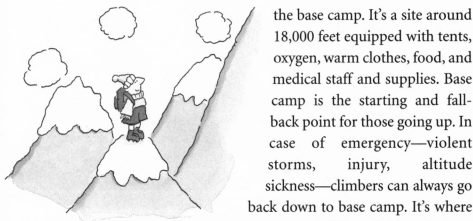

Your organization needs a good base camp. Your role as leader requires that you give your organization the systems and procedures needed for the arduous climb ahead. Like getting to the top of Everest, getting to the top of the financial services industry requires producers follow the path other producers have blazed before them. The keys to any good organizational environment are the systems you, as a leader, create to replicate success among your producers.

After you find a qualified candidate, you have an opportunity to show your true colors. The weak manager coaxes, "Come with me . . . I will get you a higher payout for the same production." Strong leaders help producers become better than ever before, produce at higher levels, and create a better life. They don't require workaholism. They have the systems; they have the experience; they have the track record. They don't coax; they *attract.* But they are interested only in coaching someone who is as ready to get to work as they are. And wouldn't you know it? That's who *wants* to work with them.

TRANSITIONING A PRODUCER FROM ANOTHER FIRM

When you and a producer decide it's time for him or her to leave another company and join your team, it's important that you demonstrate how working with you will be different from the outset:

Leader.   Dale, it's been a delight getting to know you. I have truly enjoyed learning about you and your business. You have some exciting aspirations. I think it has become evident during our

(continued next page)

---

discussions that, as successful as you may be, you are operating well below your capacity. Your Success Road Map indicates significant possibilities. I would like to have the opportunity to help you make what's on your map a reality so you move to the next level of success. Are you interested in seriously discussing making a transition to our firm so we can work together to make that happen?

Candidate. Yes, that's why I came to you.

Leader. Terrific. I am not interested in having you simply transfer your current clients from your existing firm so we get your production. I have a plan to help you experience a significant increase in production and quality of life as a result of the move. This is going to require your commitment and dedicated follow-through.

We have a transition team [*or process*] so transferring the accounts is the easy part. More important, we expect your total commitment, both personally and financially. There are several training programs we want you to enroll in. We will support you in getting the ideas you learn implemented so you can experience a significant increase in your business. Here's how it works . . .

This is where you explain the details of the plan. Remember, it's appropriate that your strategy be detailed and in writing, much like a financial plan is written by an advisor for a client. At the same time, you can explain the details. Here's an example:

Leader.   I have identified the four highest priorities for you to focus on:

1) You are seeing too many people below the quality you should be seeking. The first thing we are going to do is set a higher target client profile and identify your existing clients who meet that profile. This will increase the amount of revenue per client.

2) You have a "wing-it" client interview style that can be greatly improved. We are going to plug you into a training program that will teach you how to conduct high-trust client interviews using a Financial Road Map similar to the Success Road Map you and I used to build our relationship. This will shorten the time it takes for clients to do business with you and attract all of their assets instead of just making a sale. This will also position you as their trusted advisor so they will be more comfortable referring you to their family, friends, and colleagues.

3) Once you have a clear target client profile and have perfected your interview skills, we are going to teach you how to effectively ask for and consistently get referrals from your best clients.

4) You spend too much time doing administrative work. We are going to put you into a training program that will help you be more effective at delegating and hiring qualified people for delegation. This will give you more free time to enjoy your new, super-productive life.

There's more to do than these first four things I have outlined, but this should give you a

(continued next page)

50–100% increase in production in the first year—*if* you really follow the program. And if you come to work with us, we will ask you to sign a commitment letter pledging to implement your action plan.

How do you like it so far?

Candidate. It looks fantastic. Can you really help me make this happen?

Leader. This is the business we're in. We do it all the time. When do you want to get started?

Candidate. How soon can I get started?

Leader. I have the paperwork right here.
[*Or if the candidate wants to get back to you:*]
Of course you can think it over. But don't take too long. The longer you wait, the more I'll wonder how serious you are about taking your business and life to the highest level. How long would you like to have to think it over?

Candidate. Just a few days. Can I call you next Monday?

Leader. That will be fine. I look forward to hearing from you Monday.

If you have no track record of helping producers double their production and have a better quality of life, what should you do? Pretend? No. Your first task is to perfect your systems and your ability to get your existing producers to implement them. Remarkably, when you have an organization where most of the producers are more successful than those at other organizations, guess who does your "recruiting" for you. That's right: your producers and your reputation. An organization of just one high-performance producer who's a result of your systems and coaching is a better recruiting magnet than several producers with mediocre results.

We repeat: *If you cannot honestly make this claim—if you do not have the systems, the experience, and the track record—then the first place to focus is on yourself and your existing producers.* If you can't yet hire the right people and make them successful, then why on earth would you be recruiting more people? The high-trust leader isn't playing the numbers game. The high-trust leader is building a successful organization by helping producers succeed.

You simply cannot run an effective organization without systems. First of all, in every organization, more than one person is responsible for leadership and management responsibilities. If they are not unified by a system, the people who are being led or trained get different messages from different individuals at different times. Not only is this confusing, but it also teaches producers to keep asking the same question of different people until they get the answer they want to hear. This is clearly counterproductive, so it's extremely important from a purely organizational and morale standpoint that there be consistency.

Second, if every procedure were left to the individual practitioner, whether manager or producer, then you couldn't build a real culture or develop a methodology that has the advantage of being reinforced by peer pressure within the organization.

On the other hand, if everyone is doing essentially the same thing, meeting certain minimal standards in each aspect of their careers, a new person joining the organization naturally strives to measure up and fit in. Consistent systems, consistent culture, consistent performance.

When new individuals are brought on board, they undergo some form of training. Each component of that training should presume that everybody in the organization will have experienced the same procedures. Concurrently, you need systems for the

Consistent systems, consistent culture, consistent performance.

staff, with specific areas of responsibility and standardized procedures for carrying out the work. The same applies to bookkeeping, cost controls, budgeting, compliance, and so on. The point is that everything is standardized.

That's not to say we'll prescribe your standardized system here. There is no such thing as an industry-wide system that you can apply to your organization. The reason we won't assign specific details is that no two organizations are alike; no two organizations will have identical systems. The leader must assess the organization's structure and other factors.

◆ *What are the demographics of the people in my organization as well as its target markets?*

◆ *What special value do we offer?*

◆ *Do we represent one company or type of product, or are we a multiple-company, full-service organization?*

◆ *What are my strengths and weaknesses as a leader?*

◆ *What are our year-long and longer-range plans?*

◆ *What is our mission?*

Once these questions are answered, you have to determine what will be the necessary support for the organization. This includes developing a staff and management team that buys into the mission statement and understands the direction of the organization. They, along with producers, can then help you formulate an approach to the marketplace.

Clearly, the system for success is almost never defined in the same terms by leaders of different organizations. What doesn't change is the fact that you and your organization *must have* systems. Accountability of the leader plays a big part in making any system work. If you are to create mutual loyalty and a high-trust relationship with your producers, you must accept a greater degree of accountability for making them successful.

When you hire people, you tell them you can help them build the type of life they want. As you help them establish their dreams, values, and goals you say, both implicitly and explicitly, "Come to work with me and I'll mentor and coach you to make all your dreams come true."

As a leader you are accountable for combining office, client relationship, and marketing micro-systems to create an overall macrosystem for your producers' success. Of course, this macrosystem must be customized for each person, yet the principles of your overall success system remain the same. You will use what you've discovered in creating the Success Road Map to determine which parts of your microsystems will be combined to create a macrosystem for the success of the individual producer. This customized system must encompass many aspects: connecting with his or her natural market; advice on how to dress, how to behave professionally, how to organize an office, how to hire a staff person; managing the database, etc.

In addition to mapping out operational and information systems, you must also be clear about the system for attracting and establishing high-trust relationships with clients—behaviors that, done consistently, lead to a higher degree of success. A good place to start is with a *behavior checklist* that gives the producer a crystal-clear picture of what is required every day. This begins with a simple conversation that is supportive yet blunt:

> *The following are the behaviors that have to be executed daily for you to be successful, and within this interactive system I'll be your coach and help you consistently execute them. When you're doing well, I'll point it out so you can continue. But when I see your behavior is inconsistent with the desired outcome, I'll be accountable for letting you know and helping you change it. If at some time you can't or won't use the system I've given you, I hope you'll save me the trouble of firing you and resign.*

What does the behavior checklist or commitment letter look like? It's not a bunch of legal mumbo jumbo. It can be as simple as two columns on a piece of paper: On the left is written what the candidate is going to do, on the right what the leader and the firm is going to do, and on the bottom are both signatures. It's a simple declaration you can both return to in order to hold one another accountable to implementation. And implementation is the name of the game. That's what produces results.

This stark accountability requires a high-touch interaction between leader and producer. The traditional role of manager is to push and cajole people into producing. The high-trust leader acts more as coach and mentor. This relationship requires the leader to focus on the success of the producer and use experience, expertise, and established systems for success to lead the producer toward meeting goals.

Mentoring and coaching like this are the foundation on which great leaders and great people are built. Mozart had his father. Thomas Jefferson had the man who taught him law, George Mason. Helen Keller had her teacher, Anne Sullivan. Think of how many people have affected your life thus far. Perhaps a parent or grandparent, a teacher or sports coach, perhaps a minister or rabbi. It could be you've emulated a famous figure like Mozart, Jefferson, or Keller. We're willing to bet there's someone in your life who has helped shape you into the person you are today. Your financial services organization is the same. In this case, as a high-trust leader you are *de facto* the mentor and role model.

BE A ROLE MODEL

As a leader, you have to realize that it's true: People won't do as you say, but they'll do as you do. No matter what you tell them, they're observing your daily activities, and they're either going to use you as an excuse for mediocrity or emulate your excellence. If you want the people around you to be extraordinary, you've got to be extraordinary yourself.

The systems you've created are the systems your producers will implement. It is your success they will emulate. It is your lead they will follow. If you approach your producers as a mentor and coach, instead of as a traditional manager, you'll find you have a special relationship in which both leader and producer have ownership (are both part of) the success of the producer. This is high-trust leadership.

Remember, your organization is a team made up of strong, capable individuals who have a driving desire to succeed. As a coach you must understand them before you can lead them. For you to create this type of high-trust relationship, you'll need some important tools. As we've stressed in the last few chapters, recruiting is the first step and hiring is the second; developing a binding relationship is the next. To get you to this point we're offering samples of the 1) in-depth interview, 2) pre-career program, and 3) job offer, as well as tips for establishing a high-trust relationship.

The In-Depth Interview

As we stressed in earlier chapters, hiring is crucial to a highly productive organization. The *in-depth interview* is actually a series of interviews that qualify the candidate to go into the pre-career phase (if you have one). After a Non-Interview, which is an informal social interaction, you can schedule the first interview in the series.

First Interview—This first meeting might involve all or some of the following: the Values Conversation, the Career Rater, the Success Road Map, and aptitude tests.

Second Interview—Now you can ask the candidate to complete what we call *Project 100,* in which they write down at least 100 names of people to talk to— not prospects, just names of people to call on the telephone and have a conversation about anything. After explaining the process, you introduce them to other producers in the office and some have candid one-on-one meetings with the candidate behind closed doors with you out of the way.

Third Interview—By this time you should have their aptitude scores and their Project 100, they've met people in your organization, people in the organization have had a chance get a gut feeling about them, and you've decided to proceed. This is when you reveal the downside of the business. Open up and tell them about how hard the work can be, the difficulties of prospecting, and call-reluctance and rejection.

Make it very clear there are negatives and challenges involved in this business, and reinforce your organizational structure and goal of providing the base camp for overcoming these challenges and combating the negatives.

If the candidate is married, you may want to include the spouse in this interview. We believe it's vital for the candidate to know the truths about the business and to be secure in his or her decision to join the organization. For some, it may be important to consult with or even have the approval of a spouse; in that case, we suggest you accommodate and give both the candidate and the spouse the information and exposure to your organization necessary to make a united decision. In any relationship, both people will be affected by this business, so we suggest you always respect the wishes of the candidate to involve a spouse at this point.

Evaluation—After this interview, you should complete an evaluation of the recruit on a form like the one on page 117. This is important because it graphically represents what may still just be indistinct impressions. Take a good long look at your answers and remember: the numbers don't lie.

NEW RECRUIT EVALUATION

Name _____ Supervisor's Name _____

Next School _____

Potential Contract Date _____ (surveys completed)

Natural Market: ($50,000 or more of income only)

Superior	200 +	(50–75 at $100,000)
Good	100 +	(30–50 at $100,000)
Average	75 +	(15–30 at $100,000)
Below Avg.	50 +	(1–15 at $100,000)
Poor	Less than 40	

Finances:	**Income**	**Liquidity**	**Net Worth**
Superior	$100,000 +	$75,000 +	$ 400,000 +
Good	75,000 +	40,000 +	250,000 +
Average	50,000 +	20,000 +	125,000 +
Below Avg.	35,000 +	10,000 +	50,000 +
Poor	20,000 +	Less than 10,000 +	Less than 50,000 +

Geographic Stability

Superior	15 years +
Good	10 years +
Average	5 years +
Below Avg.	2 years +
Poor	Less than 2 years

	SUPERIOR	GOOD	AVERAGE	BELOW AVERAGE	POOR	SCORE	COMMENTS
1. Penetrable Natural Market (10–7–4–2–0)							
2. Finances (10–7–4–2–0)							
3. Achievement Background (8–6–4–2–1)							
4. Career Relevancy (8–6–4–2–1)							
5. Appearance (5–4–3–2–1)							
6. Career Stability (5–4–3–2–1)							
7. Personal Stability (5–4–3–2–1)							
8. Educational Relevancy (5–4–3–2–1)							
9. Geographic Stability (5–4–3–2–1)							
10. Organizational Compatability (5–4–3–2–1)							
11. Aptitude Test Scores (5–4–3–2–1)							

Total Score ____

Rating	
Superior	56–71
Good	43–55
Average	30–42
Below Avg.	21–29
Poor	9–20

The Pre-Career Program

Once you have a qualified candidate, training can be conducted over a period of time or can be a formal, several-months-long process called the pre-career program. This type of program is the final stage, the last chance to turn back. In this program you can intensify the questioning and ask candidates to stretch themselves in two distinct areas: identifying and contacting their warm markets.

MAKING THE OFFER

Following are two types of invitations to join the firm. They are offered as illustrations only, not as scripts. Of course, you'll want to tailor this to your own style, but the essence of the offer is always the same: "You are an excellent candidate . . . We are interested in you . . . Here's what it will take to join us . . . Are you interested?"

Dale, it's been a delight. I've come to the conclusion from our meetings that you have the capacity to be outstanding in our business. And not only that, our business would probably give you more reward and more opportunity to achieve your own personal dreams than you could find anywhere else. But all that notwithstanding, I believe to be fair to you and our organization we need to take this a step further. I'm not going to try to get you into this business and then have you find out you made a mistake. So, the way we make sure this is right for you and right for us is to have you enter our pre-career program. What that means is we put you into an accelerated learning situation in which you learn about the business and we learn about you. We'll team you up with our people, train you, educate you, and help you get any licensing you may need, all at no cost to you.

All I ask is that you go into this training program with total commitment to give it your best shot. If you complete everything in the process and believe this is right for you, since I've already made up my mind that you have the capacity, we will begin your new professional career.

The process takes about two to three months and can be done part-time. Keep your current job and at any time if you feel this is not right for you, you can back out. But if it's right I guarantee it'll be the greatest decision you've ever made. Now, are you prepared to begin?

NOTE: If you decide you want to make a full-time commitment to new producers without a pre-career program, this type of introduction to the firm would still make sense. Simply eliminate the contingency language:

Dale, it's been a delight. I've come to the conclusion from our meetings that you are someone who will be very successful in our business. The next step is for you to come to work with our firm. You will attend our training school where you will get your licensing, develop your product knowledge, and create a marketing plan. This is a full-time commitment, and we will pay you $X during the training period. [Explain your company's compensation package and transition from subsidy to full commission/fee income.] Have you decided to join us?

On pages 120–121, you'll find a *Who Do You Know?* form. This is a tool to get the candidate to create a potential client list. In one pre-career program, candidates are required to complete at least twenty-five prospective client visits, using the *Who Do You Know?* as a guide. This reveals whether the candidate has the fortitude to pick up the phone, the discipline to go and see the person, and the capacity to get that person to answer the questions. It's a test to see if the candidate can complete the process. Similarly, the *Confidential Survey* on pages 122–123 requests the candidate to complete a structured interview with contacts and then attempt to get a list of references of at least three people as potential clients.

WHO DO YOU KNOW?

Candidate/Producer _____ Date _____

Consider those in . . .

Business Machine or Computer Sales

Pharmaceutical/Hospital Supply Sales

Advertising Sales—newspaper, radio, TV, magazine, etc.

Brokerage Sales*—stocks, bonds, mutual funds, etc.

Real Estate—residential or commercial

Banker—dissatisfied

Attorney—dissatisfied

Teacher or Coach

General—automobiles. clothing, furniture, etc.

Who is the most successful salesperson you know in the area?

Can you recommend a person who is successful like yourself?

*preferably in this profession *less* than 3–5 years

Name	Occupation	Age	Telephone	Address
1.			W = H =	
2.			W = H =	
3.			W = H =	
4.			W = H =	
5.			W = H =	
6.			W = H =	
7.			W = H =	
8.			W = H =	
9.			W = H =	
10.			W = H =	
11.			W = H =	
12.			W = H =	
13.			W = H =	
14.			W = H =	
15.			W = H =	
16.			W = H =	

CONFIDENTIAL SURVEY

Name _____ Date of Birth _____ Time Known _____

Address _____ Phone _____

Occupation _____ Phone _____

Family Status: Single ___ Married ___ Spouse's Name _____ No. of Children ____

1. What does the term "financial planning" mean to you? _____
   _____
   _____

2. What is your opinion of a career in financial services? _____
   _____

3. In today's economy what investments do you feel perform well? _____
   _____

4. What investments do you own or plan to purchase in the near future? _____
   _____

5. Do you feel obligated to buy future investments from the same salesperson? _____
   Yes ___ No ___ Why? _____
   _____

6. Do you believe in life insurance? Yes ___ No ___ Why? _____
   _____

7. How much life insurance do you own? $ _____ Spouse $ _____ Children $ _____
   _____

8. Why did you buy your program? _____

9. How much are your life insurance premiums? Annually $ _____ /or Monthly ? _____

10. Do you feel obligated to buy your next policy from the same salesperson? _____
    Yes ___ No ___ Why? _____

11. Do you have a health insurance plan? Yes _____ No _____

    Privately owned _____ At work _____ Satisfied _____

12. Do you have a disability program? Yes _____ No _____

    Privately owned _____ At work _____

13. Are you happy with your present homeowners/auto insurance? Yes _____ No _____

14. At what age do you expect to retire? _____ Why? _____

15. Do you have a retirement plan?
    IRA   Yes ____ No _____ How Invested _____
    Keogh Plan   Yes ____ No _____ How Invested _____
    Pension Plan   Yes ___ No _____ How Invested _____
    Profit Sharing Plan   Yes ___ No _____ How Invested _____
    Annual Contribution Amount $ _____

16. Do you and your spouse have wills or trusts?

    Yes _____ No ____ Last Updated _____

17. Your approximate tax bracket _____

18. Do you have any plans for any business venture in the future? _____

19. Approximately, from all sources, what might your income be this year? $ _____

    Spouse's $ _____

20. If I joined Tip-Top Financial Group, would you agree to a meeting in the future allowing me to show their products and services?

    Yes ____ No ____ Why? _____

21. Again, if I joined Tip-Top Financial Group, who are *three* people you would recommend I call?

Name	Occupation	Address	Phone

This and previous chapters have offered you a number of tools to use in the recruiting and training process. In the next few chapters, we will focus on helping producers implement your ideas to achieve their dreams. The future requires bold leaders who are not afraid to lead people to reach their own goals and aspirations. In an age of increased individual responsibility and entrepreneurialism, the successful high-trust leader is the one who helps people help themselves.

TIPS FOR ESTABLISHING HIGH-TRUST RELATIONSHIPS

◆ Know the values, goals, wants, aspirations, and dreams of the producer.

◆ Enroll in helping the producer reach those goals. This requires not only a personal commitment, but also a relationship in which you announce your intended partnering (coaching/ mentoring) to the producer.

◆ Become a coach and mentor. This type of relationship is, by nature, one of partnering and teaching the producer to reach his or her goals. Those goals may include any or all areas of the producer's life: finances, home, children, marriage, emotion, spirituality. Coaching requires a greater degree of trust on the part of both the leader and the producer. It is the building of this trust that creates a loyal relationship. Loyalty is the key to the success of the individual producer and, in turn, the organization.

◆ Take accountability for the success of producers. As their coach and mentor you must establish systems to guarantee success.

This system and the microsystems that make it up includes a behavior checklist—the behaviors needed for success. The leader must be willing to let producers know when they are not displaying that behavior and partner with the producer to get back on track. Of course, such accountability requires you to recognize when a producer cannot or will not use the systems and take steps to protect the organization.

◆ Make people your business. Spend your time and energy as a leader working *for* your producers. Make their success your goal.

CHAPTER 7

The High-Trust Culture:
Creating and Protecting
an Environment for Success

> If I have seen further . . .
> it is by standing upon the
> shoulders of giants.
>
> SIR ISAAC NEWTON

First there was Socrates, then Plato, Aristotle, and finally Alexander the Great. This relatively long line of men who challenged and encouraged others into greatness demonstrates the power of high-trust leadership. Each directly influenced the next, inspiring others to their own highest level of success.

The ancient concepts of leadership tend to conjure images of one invincible visionary charging a hill with loyal troops behind. Yet any leader today knows how romanticized this is. Those who fancy themselves a modern-day Tom, Dick, or Harriet the Great have lost sight of the behind-the-scenes preparations, teamwork, and, frankly, tedium that goes into any moment of glory.

Even our contemporary models of leadership, in this industry especially, have grown outmoded. Once upon a time, producer-leaders set the pace for the organization, outselling and outperforming others, pulling them along by sheer force of will and an indomitable spirit. All leaders had to do then was set some outrageous goals, work their tails off, help when necessary, and watch their producers either fall in line or fall out. It wasn't necessarily easy, but it was simple. Today, most of us are confronted with too many complex concerns—compliance, competition, costs, etc.—to be both the star producer and the leader of an effective organization. We've had to find a new way of leading, yet our intent remains the same: show 'em the way and let 'em run with it. *Follow me, and I'll bring out the best in you.* Like Socrates, Plato, and Aristotle, we inspire others to equal or even surpass our accomplishments.

This is a tactic that hails, remarkably enough, from the Marines. It's remarkable because it eschews the "I'm-in-charge-and-you're-not" mentality associated with many military styles. Instead, "warfighting," which is what the Marines call it, requires the commanding officer to set a goal and parameters, then empower the platoon leaders down to the lowest rank to make command decisions. It relies on the grit and determination of every soldier. Warfighting translates easily to business and has been adopted as an aggressive, progressive, take-no-prisoners style ideally suited to the dynamic self-starter, who can be anywhere from the top of the organization all the way down. The leader designs a culture or environment of achievement based on a shared desire to see the producers, the leader, and the company achieve stated goals. High-trust leaders rely heavily on the selection and recruiting process to hire only the most motivated people, the people most likely to succeed in this environment. These leaders then create a culture where producers can thrive by coaching them to reach their goals and respecting individual values.

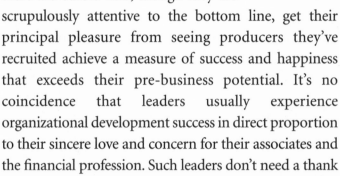

At the heart of such a culture is, as you might guess, an abiding level of trust. In examining your own capacity to create a culture founded on trust and built with respect and coaching, you might take a look at why you went into management in the first place. Some managers are turned on only by profit, production, prestige, and so on. Yet there are others who, though they are scrupulously attentive to the bottom line, get their principal pleasure from seeing producers they've recruited achieve a measure of success and happiness that exceeds their pre-business potential. It's no coincidence that leaders usually experience organizational development success in direct proportion to their sincere love and concern for their associates and the financial profession. Such leaders don't need a thank

---

It's no coincidence that leaders usually experience organizational development success in direct proportion to their sincere love and concern for their associates and the financial profession.

---

you or a big profit to feel the intense pleasure of success, but both are usually forthcoming. It's no great task for them to give generously of their time and expertise to producers, because that is what makes them tick. The leader who doesn't really care will be hard pressed to sustain a long career of producer development with the necessary enthusiasm. And such an attitude is counterproductive to high-trust leadership.

Of course, attitude is necessary but not sufficient by itself. For autonomous management to work, the leader must diligently preserve the culture (which is de-centralized, independent, self-driving), explicitly state goals, and clearly define parameters. Every person in the organization must be committed to excellence and personally responsible for his or her own success. Each must "own" the organizational goals as well as his or her personal goals. This type of management also requires a certain organizational structure, one that allows the leader and producers some freedoms, although some practical restrictions are enforced.

Just as the CEO of a company has to follow the dictates of a board of directors or, at the very least, federal and state laws, the leader of a financial services company of any size has to operate within industry regulations, as does every person who works in that organization. Whether you are the leader of a company, or a regional or satellite office, there are certain restrictions handed down from "on high." Everyone lives with constraints; the question is not how to get around them but how to rigidly follow them while you distinguish yourself and your entire producer group by performing at your highest levels.

Think this is difficult? It may be, but that doesn't make it impossible, and the rewards are huge. Consider the accomplishments of John Norquist, mayor of Milwaukee. Perhaps nowhere else is the bureaucratic maze more convoluted than in politics, but Norquist manages to work within the confines of government while thinking and acting "outside the box." He's an unusual mix, a popular Democrat whose focus is on the bottom line. Approaching the revitalization of his city with entrepreneurial zeal, in ten years he has committed himself to, in his words, raising quality and not just spending money. Rare sentiments for a politician. Even more rare are his results: Every year in office, he cut the city's tax rates; during his tenure he cut city expenditures by more than 20% so the city was actually spending money at a rate at or below the rate of inflation; and he's cut the city's payroll by 10%. The list goes on, with positive changes not only in the fiscal realm but also in the areas of unemployment, property values, crime, and wages.

How does this example translate to our industry? Norquist is a regional leader encumbered with a number of restrictions and myriad responsibilities; his success is measured in tangible results; and his achievements depend on the cooperation of a large organization. He has adopted an attitude that we encourage you to take as your own: Regardless of your actual job title, act and think like a chief executive officer.

Preserving the Culture

In a high-trust organization, the leader inspires every individual to think like an entrepreneur. Every producer becomes the "CEO" of his or her own domain, just as you are in control of yours. This can yield phenomenal results, especially in the financial services industry, because many of the people who are attracted to this kind of career find it appealing precisely because it allows them to be more enterprising:

- ◆ Income is commensurate with results;
- ◆ No financial or career ceiling exists;
- ◆ Work styles are independent;
- ◆ The leader is more a committed partner than boss;
- ◆ The work environment provides a "base camp" for encouragement, help, and security;
- ◆ The workforce has a greater sense of ownership in the company.

We live in interesting times, when top professionals leave their careers for a variety of reasons, including a desire for any of the above, corporate downsizing, relocation, etc. These already-successful individuals are prime candidates for recruiting and can provide both a new perspective and an added boost of ambition in any organization. We also have the unique opportunity to work with those who have not yet achieved high levels of success, our "diamonds in the rough." Individuals in our line of work can raise themselves to whatever height they are prepared to pay the price to reach, and people from every segment of the community can be suitable recruits. There is perhaps no greater management experience than seeing someone create a new life for himself or herself simply by embarking on a new career path.

Many years ago, Norman had just such an opportunity. A Russian immigrant walked into his office to convey, in broken English, that he was a political refugee and (after taking some aptitude tests through a Russian-American charity) had decided that selling was the career for him. Against every rule in the book, but based on some strong gut reactions, this fellow was brought into a pre-career program. He had a sparkle in his eye, tremendous ambition and desire— and no contacts. Yet during the pre-career period, he did even better than expected, gracefully managing the transition to the American culture and a brand-new business. He was selling to other immigrants, primarily in Russian, but his English was improving. He was very bright, learned quickly, and was promptly hired after the pre-career period concluded. He qualified for the Million Dollar Round Table (MDRT) within a year, and as of this writing he's still with the agency as one of its top producers. He has brought others into the agency, too, among them two more Russian immigrants who have made a new life for themselves with him as a valued mentor.

Obviously, not every leader can sit and wait for such a person to waltz into the office. In fact, you'd be taking a big risk by hiring someone like this, but it's occasionally worth it. If you want to find excellent possibilities, the top people to consider are as follows:

- Those with fine educational and work experience, such as professionals (accountants, lawyers, etc.) and business owners who have not been financially successful in their chosen careers. Look for people who have the right instincts but have not made it work on their own.

- First-generation Americans with a solid work discipline and stars in their eyes. Especially consider those who value free enterprise but lack an opportunity.

◆ Those who come from a disadvantaged background but have overcome their financial, physical, or educational obstacles and are seeking an opportunity to excel.

KEEP YOUR EYE ON THE BIG PICTURE.

Don't get bogged down in the minutiae or carried away by irrelevant activities. Being busy is not the hallmark of a great leader; doing what helps your producers is. We know of one manager, tremendously skilled with the technical side of the business and marginal with the rest, who illustrates what *not* to do flawlessly. A prime case in point is the time he got a parking ticket. In those days, it was a meager $5 to settle the fine and get on with his life. But he thought it was unjustified and decided to go to court. So he took a day off and, wouldn't you know it? His "big case" was postponed until the next day. So he took a second day off to fight the $5 ticket. He argued that it was the principle of the thing, but he wound up losing the case anyway, paying the $5, and costing himself two days in the process. This may seem trivial, but it's telling. Can you think of instances where you or the people who work with you have gotten sucked into these costly little dramas? Your job is to set the example and focus on what's important.

Any individual who has the ability to see the value of a career in financial services is ripe for a discussion with you, and you may find that some of the best candidates are those who can ill afford to sink time or money into much further education. Just remember that you are looking for people who will *add* to the culture of achievement you have already established. Your primary goal is to foster that culture. Balance your zeal for production with your long-range plans for a top-notch organization.

CHAPTER 8.

Beyond Goal Setting:
Helping Producers Build Themselves
as You Build Your Business

> He that would have the fruit
> must climb the tree.
>
> THOMAS FULLER, M.D.

We're sure you've heard the one about the man who comes out of a bar late one night and spies a man on his knees under a lamppost.

"Excuse me sir," he says. "What are you doing?"

The man on his knees stops, looks up, and explains, "I'm looking for my car keys."

"Oh, I see, where do you think you dropped them? Maybe I can help," the man offers.

"I'm pretty sure I dropped them over there," the other man says, pointing to the dark side of the parking lot.

"Uh, sir, if you dropped your keys way over there why are you looking for them here under this lamppost?"

"Because this is where the light is."

Although you may not meet a producer quite so far off the mark, most need your guidance and leadership to find the keys to their success. As a leader you have the awesome responsibility and accountability to create and protect the culture for your organization. This may sound like a daunting task; however, we've found it to be an acheivable process that begins with goal setting and progresses into the personal development of the leader and producer.

Stating Goals

One of the first jobs of the leader is to clearly state organizational goals. Because in day-to-day operations you cannot micromanage your producers or other staff (the absence of micromanagement is a defining factor of high-trust leadership), you must feel confident that they know where they're headed.

It's inappropriate for us to suggest the proper goals for your organization in this book; they are wholly unique, just as each individual's goals vary. Yet one rule of thumb should always be followed: *Have a big goal.* In fact, if you are serious about creating a top organization, have a completely outrageous goal. In the book *Built to Last,* Stanford professors Jerry Porras and James Collins found the most successful and long-lasting companies in America had a number of things in common. Number one on the list? They set BHAGs: Big Hairy Audacious Goals. Somewhat more eloquently, George Bernard Shaw observed, "All progress depends on the unreasonable man."

A tool generally used to establish and express individual producers' goals that may also work well for illustrating organizational goals is the Success Road Map explained earlier in Chapter 5. This tool would provide a visual representation of your company's current situation, desired future, and the steps necessary to arrive there. Every producer should have a personal Success Road Map, and you should have a copy in your files for reference in conducting one-on-one meetings. It should go without saying that the producers' goals must be an extension of the organizational goals (e.g., minimum production goals should reflect the minimum production target for the organization), but in most cases the producers' goals should exceed those minimums—and their performance *must* exceed them.

The Nine Core Competencies of a Successful Producer

You have already helped your producer identify personal goals—now you need to coach him or her in setting some professional goals. We've identified Nine Core Competencies as crucial to the development of a successful producer. Not only will these help guide producers and provide further dimension to the behavior contract (you could even incorporate these into that document if you wished), but they will also keep producers focused on what really matters. There will be no time for complaining or blaming or excuse making because they will be so busy working on themselves.

The leader should walk producers through these competencies, helping them rate themselves on a scale of 1–10. Below we've also provided a rough guide to the scale (pages 140–146) and a worksheet (page 148) for reviewing the competencies with producers. When the worksheet is completed, the leader should help the producer go back and prioritize the competencies (A, B, C, etc.) so it's clear which one is most important.

A 10 represents the ideal attitude and preparation a producer can have. We've called the 10s our *Top Producers* because they are the paragons of the Nine Core Competencies. The *Most Producers* of this guide are where the majority find themselves (usually in the 1–4 range). Your job as leader is to help these average producers become 10s.

Competency One—Develop a clear, focused business/marketing/sales plan. This includes the master plan, defined target market, creation of strategic alliances, and the process of growing to the amount and form of compensation you and the producer desire.

What it sounds like:

Leader:

> *Do you have a business plan?*
> *A marketing plan? A sales plan?*

Most producers:

> *I don't exactly have a "business plan." I do have goals, if that's what you mean.*

Top producers:

> *Yes, I have a written business plan that outlines where I am now and where I want to be in the future. I also have a written plan of how I will approach my target market. My sales plan is the system my manager has taught me for creating high-trust relationships with new clients.*

Competency Two—Focus on producing results and delegate everything else to capable support staff.

Leader:

> *Do you have a capable support staff—*
> *people to whom you delegate everything*
> *that does not directly affect relationships*
> *with clients and potential clients?*

Most producers:

> *No. I do everything myself. I just don't have*
> *time to show someone else how to do it.*

Top producers:

> *Of course I have a staff I've cultivated and*
> *who are capable of doing anything I send*
> *their way. I stay completely focused on my*
> *clients.*

Competency Three—Become brilliant at building high-trust client relationships, especially in the first interview. Producers know they're "brilliant" when clients tell them where their assets are, follow their advice, do all the prospecting and marketing for them, and are more influenced by them than by friends, family or the media.

Leader:

> *Do prospects come to your office with all*
> *their documents and, by the end of the first*
> *hour-long interview, do you usually get*
> *hired?*

Most producers:

> *Not exactly. I have to have several meetings
> and phone calls before I get to yes or no.
> And I ususally just focus on one sale at a
> time, then "drip" on them to get more
> business over time.*

Top producers:

> *I have a very comprehensive first interview.
> My staff helps my prospects get everything
> together for the first meeting. When we
> meet, the interview is structured and the
> emphasis is much more on building trust
> and establishing a fit versus me trying to
> make a sale to fill a need. If I choose to
> invite them to become a client and if they
> choose to hire me, then I create a
> comprehensive plan relative to the services I
> offer. What I charge and how I am paid are
> discussed up front. Without a solid
> commitment from my prospect to
> implement my recommendations I do not
> proceed.*

Competency Four—Master referral-based business development.

Leader:

> *What percentage of your new business
> comes to you through referral? (100% of
> your clients=10, 90%=9, and so on.)*

Most producers:

> *Uh, I'm not sure. Most of my business comes from . . . I'm not sure.*

Top producers:

> *I used to spend a lot of money on direct mail, seminars, and even had cold-callers, but I don't do any of that any more. I still send ideas of value to my clients and do client appreciation seminars, but all of my new business comes from referrals: 100%.*

Competency Five—Work as hard on developing yourself as you do on developing your business.

Leader:

> *What was the last personal development book or audio cassette you read? What was the last seminar you attended? Do you have a mentor?*

Most producers:

> *I don't read many books. One by Tom Clancy once in a while. The last seminar I attended was year before last and my boss made me go to that one. What do you mean by a mentor?*

Top producers:

> *I read at least one personal development book every month and I keep audio cassettes in my car so I can listen to them as I travel. I attend seminars at least once each*

quarter. My mentor is a colleague who is part of my "mastermind"/study group.

Competency Six—Operate your business efficiently, so you are running it instead of it running you.

Leader:

How much free time do you have? Do you exercise regularly? When was the last time you apologized to your family for not being able to do something with them because of your business obligations?

Most producers:

It's been a long time since I had a weekend free. It seems like I'm always running from the office to some business function, then home to sleep, then I start all over again. Am I supposed to have free time?

Top producers:

I spend as much time with my family as I like. I make all my daughter's basketball games and my spouse and I go out at least two nights each week for "date night." I also work out three to five days a week. My faith is important to me, and I volunteer quite a bit of time to my place of worship.

Competency Seven—Become a master of time, especially in managing weekly and daily priorities.

Leader:

Show me your day planner or your personal digital assistant. Are your tasks scheduled and prioritized? Does your schedule support your goals (i.e., does it help you spend more time with clients and less with paper)?

Most producers:

Well I have this calendar and sometimes I make a to-do list, or else I put these sticky-notes in here as reminders. I keep most everything in my head.

Top producers:

I have a good grasp of time management. In fact, I have a planner I keep and use religiously. Each task and meeting is recorded and prioritized. It also acts as a support tool for my personal goals. Here, let me show you . . .

Competency Eight—Build a computer-based business and marketing infrastructure, and/or learn and *use* what your company provides. This infrastructure is what facilitates consistent prospect contact, professional client service, and the implementation of successful marketing strategies.

Leader:

Do you have a computer-based system for running your business and helping you market yourself?

Most producers:

I have a computer, but I use it mostly for playing CD-ROM golf.

Top Producers:

> *Yes, I have a great software program I use to fully manage my office and business operations. I also have a software program that helps me keep track of all my customers. It prompts me to contact them on a regular basis and helps keep me informed about their buying habits and special needs.*

Competency Nine—Become a better financial professional. By truly becoming great at the craft of helping people make smart financial choices you will attract the best clients rather than pursue them.

Leader:

> *Do you consistently improve your skills, earn new designations, and upgrade your understanding of all factors influencing your industry?*

Most producers:

> *Yeah, kinda. I read the trades and belong to a professional organization.*

Top producers:

> *Yes, I have already achieved my CLU and CFP. I regularly read industry-specific material and my staff keeps careful records on changes in compliance, available products, etc. I am active in several professional organizations.*

When producers have trouble understanding any of these core competencies, you ought to be able to use yourself as an example. If they don't see how using a day planner or digital assistant will help them be more efficient, you ought to be able to show them yours to illustrate the point. If they don't know the difference between a business plan, sales plan, and marketing plan, you ought to be able to not only explain the difference but show them your organization's plans. And so on. Be sure you don't preach the old saw "Do as I say, not as I do." Instead, be a role model, an example they can respect and emulate.

On the following page is a worksheet you can use with producers in reviewing the competencies. Help them be brief in their responses to the questions; you don't need the history of their work on this competency, just where they are now. Personal development speaker Jim Rohn used to have a funny line about people who felt the need to explain their ratings in self-analysis: In the little box where you're supposed to write a number, there's no room for a story. Value the truth. "The truth shall set you free" is more than a philosophical idea; it's highly practical, too.

COMPETENCY	Rating 1–10	Resources
1. Develop a clear, focused business/marketing/sales plan.	☐	_____ _____ _____
2. Focus on producing results and delegate everything else to capable support staff.	☐	_____ _____ _____
3. Become brilliant at interpersonal relationships and client-development skills.	☐	_____ _____ _____
4. Master referral-based business development.	☐	_____ _____ _____
5. Work as hard on developing yourself as you do on developing your business.	☐	_____ _____ _____
6. Operate your business efficiently, so you are running it instead of it running you.	☐	_____ _____ _____
7. Become a master of your time, especially in managing weekly and daily priorities.	☐	_____ _____ _____
8. Build a computer-based business and marketing infrastructure, and/or learn and _use_ what your company provides.	☐	_____ _____ _____
9. Become a better financial professional.	☐	_____ _____ _____

MASTERING THE NINE CORE COMPETENCIES

As producers work to master each of these nine core competencies, they will also be building the necessary attitudes and practices of a trusted advisor, someone who not only sells products to clients, but advises them on their entire financial picture. Yet if your producers are new to the business or are not yet mature enough to handle the role and responsibilities of being a full-fledged trusted advisor, then you have a decision to make:

1) You can train new recruits as trusted advisors despite any apparent limitations (you may be pleasantly surprised), or

2) You may decide that you wish to train this producer/group of producers strictly as salespeople, restricting their interactions with clients to the sale of specific products.

Although there is no question that an organization made up entirely of trusted advisors is the wave of the future, there are varying levels of sophistication and market positioning that may influence your decision. We recognize that you have to make choices based on your reality. The last thing we want to advocate in this book is that you stop recruiting "green peas" or rookies. On the contrary. If you are reading this book, we assume you are in a position to become a high-trust leader. This doesn't necessarily assume that the people you lead are at the same level of development. We want to allow for the high-trust leader to exist in all types of organizations, including those still comprised primarily of traditional salespeople.

If you don't feel that you can groom the new producer into a trusted advisor position from the outset, you can work to mature him or her over time. There are transitional methodologies

(continued next page)

available to leaders moving producers toward the ultimate, but who are not yet there, whether it's because they don't have the confidence in the sales force yet or because the company they work with or for doesn't support it.* We recognize that you may work for a company that has mandated that you recruit twenty people a year and that it is may be unfeasible for you to recruit twenty sophisticated, mature individuals who could move beyond sales methods and into the realm of trusted advisor off the bat. That doesn't mean you wouldn't look for this kind of person or, if you found them, that you wouldn't teach them the methodologies of a trusted advisor.

If you choose to educate producers in the traditional sales methods first, the specific skills they have to learn to do are developing a market (prospecting), conducting a proper interview (learning to listen and get the facts they need on which to base a presentation), and getting people to take action (sales). Also, they need some help in time management—what's important, what's not, when they should be working, when they should be taking a vacation, where they should be spending their time while working. The premise is that weaker producers classically do a lot of things they shouldn't, don't do others they should, and don't do what they are doing as well as they could.

The precise details of the training and development we'll leave to you, of course. They will be specific to the products you represent and the producers in your organization. Yet resources for you are available, and you no doubt have some within your organization already.

— NORMAN LEVINE

*Norman Levine offers a number of materials for top sales methodologies. You can get more information by calling (800) 991-7281, or visiting the website at www.levineenterprises.com. Specifically, you can access the "High-Touch Leadership Skills" tapes for management, as well as resources for producers, such as his book *Selling With Silk Gloves, Not Brass Knuckles* (which includes the Non-Interview for salespeople) the book's companion tapes, and the "If You Sell Well, There Are No Impossible Dreams" series.

Additional Resources

In the old days, we used to do everything internally, and we could afford it. We had large staffs and lots of people in management with very specific job descriptions, with a few dedicated to training and education. That's almost impossible today. Even the largest firms have had to cut back. Simply put, some of the best resources are outside. Today, the staff must be leaner and meaner, primarily because of economics, so one of the things real leaders have learned to do is use outside resources in addition to the training and systems they have in-house.

One quick way to create a rift in your organization is to deny producers these additional resources. For example, some managers in the insurance industry may hesitate to encourage top producers to attend MDRT because they fear proselytizing. And agency or brokerage managers may discourage producers from attending any newfangled training because they are afraid it will contaminate their sales methodology. Or managers of any organization may fear exposing their people to other producers who will help them discover the strengths (and seduction) of a better organization. Yet you never lose people because of other companies; you lose them because of your own lack of the necessary interpersonal relationships. If you have developed strong, high-trust relationships with the people in your organization, producers end up with something much more compelling than additional compensation or a corner office. Using outside resources is not a risk when you are a strong leader. It's only a risk if you're not doing your job effectively. But holding your people back because you are afraid of the risk is a losing game any way you play it.

Industry involvement can be a profound help to both you and your producers. Insurance agents, stock brokers, financial planners, and other financial professionals have their own brand of industry organization. Involvement in these organizations can appear to be an end unto itself, but we view it more as a

---

You never lose people because of other companies; you lose them because of your own lack of the necessary interpersonal relationships.

---

means to education, inspiration, and innovation. Encourage your producers to participate, and get involved yourself. Both you and they will be honored and awed by the level of success others have achieved in your profession. At best, your producers will help make the industry a little better for having been there; they may become active in government, business, or local economic issues; they may accomplish a great deal more as members of a group than they ever could alone. Of course, this presumes that you care as much about the people as the production.

The key in guiding your producers to the proper organizations, independent trainers, coaches, or other programs is knowing the type of coaching they need. There are many types of coaching—including the key areas of skills, strategy/business, and accountability—

available from any number of sources. The high-trust leader recommends and supports resources and outside programs that will help producers succeed. Do they need help running their practice? Do they need to improve a specific skill set? Do they need help following through and implementing? Certainly it's different for different people. And what many producers need most is help figuring out which area they should focus on and which will have the greatest impact on their success. You can help guide them to the best sources and the most appropriate subjects. See their enthusiasm as an omen of future success; a willingness to invest in themselves is a great sign.

Having the courage to help producers find the resources they'll discover eventually anyhow and encouraging participation gives you strength. If your producers discover many more good ideas and outside resources from other producers than they do from you, watch out. This sends an unmistakable message: BREACH OF TRUST. Either you are not doing your homework, deliberately trying to hide something, or afraid of losing control. Don't let this happen to you: Care as much about finding quality resources as your producers, acknowledge that you can't really hide anything in this age of information, and realize that control is an illusion.

◆ Make sure you are teaching them current ways of creating high-trust relationships with their clients, not old-school sales techniques, and seek out the best teachers and coaches to support your producers' success.

◆ If the truth is that your producers don't need or want you, then it's just a matter of time before they discover it—and chances are they are going to discover it soon. Yet the high-trust leader is never expendable or replaceable by an outside training program, mentor, or coach.

◆ If it's better somewhere else, your producers will find out. Communism fell when the ease of communication made it simply impossible to hide the fact that everybody else was living better, or at least had the chance of living better, in the capitalist nations. The last thing you ever want to do as a producer-centered leader is try to keep things the way they have always been because it makes you comfortable, or because that's what's always worked for you, or because "it ain't broke." Successful, progressive producers will work with successful, progressive leaders. Period.

One of the best things about providing your producers with resources beyond your own organization is that you do not have to be all things to all people. You do not have to be star producer, executive, teacher, secretary, and baby-sitter all rolled into one. You can instead focus on your core function: helping producers produce. Preserving the environment. Being the catalyst. Maintaining base camp. You can finally make their success your sole objective.

One natural way to incorporate resources into your interactions with producers is to make suggestions directly relevant to specific goals or the core competencies you outline. Below is a list of resources we know; it is by no means a complete list, nor are we trying to sell you on any of these particular programs. The point is that there are so many books, tapes, workshops, and training programs that you can surely find a few that suit your organization perfectly. Avail yourself of what those people and organizations have to offer.

Target marketing/prospecting:

Successful Money Management Seminars
Wayne Cotton
Richard Weyelman
Emerald Publications

First interviews/High-trust client relationships:

Bill Bachrach

Referrals:

Mark Sheer

Running a business:

Dan Sullivan

Michael Gerber

Managing a client/prospect database:

Bill Good

Self-actualization:

Jim Rohn

Stephen Covey

Jim Cathcart

Brian Tracy

Inspiration/motivation:

Norman Levine

Nick Murray

Alan Parisse

Jim Rohn

Jack Canfield/Mark Victor Hansen

Time management:

Hyrum Smith

Alan Larkin

Alec McKenzie

Stephen Covey

Professional skills:

International Association for Financial
    Planning

Institute of Certified Financial Planners

Institute of Investment Management Consultants

Million Dollar Round Table

Securities Industry Association

Coursework to attain designations such as
    Certified Financial Planner, Certified Life

Underwriter, Chartered Financial
Consultant, Master of Science in Financial
Services, Certified Fund Specialist, etc.

In brief: Know the producer, know the competencies, know the resources. We strongly suggest you help producers make the most of their resources, both in-house and from outside sources. Encourage producers to help one another, too, in the context of study groups or working meetings where they can share what they're learning, what they think about it, and whether or not it's really helping them become more competent in the intended area. As a high-trust leader who not only talks about success but actually helps producers achieve it *by any means that is ethical and effective* you will become indispensable not only to your vendors/ parent company but to the producers, too.

CHAPTER 9.

The Seventh Generation:
Coaching to Win

> I can't understand why people
> are frightened by new ideas.
> I'm frightened of old ones.
>
> JOHN CAGE

Throughout this book we have promoted a new kind of leadership that presupposes a new kind of producer, too. With a focus on interpersonal relationships (not such a new idea but revived here), the trusted leader builds a high-performance team of trusted advisors, not an old-school organization of salespeople.

As serious students of how people sell and why people buy, both of us have observed and talked to top producers, as well as had award-winning careers as producers ourselves. The premise of this chapter is a progression or evolution of the nature of selling, which was developed by Bill and his good friend and mentor, Doug Carter. With Norman's wholehearted agreement and our individual perspectives to come, we give you the "Seven Generations of Selling."

The Evolution of Selling

First Generation—Barter, or *trade*, is the one-for-one exchange of goods between two people: "I'll trade you this animal pelt for that club."

Second Generation—A *merchant* is someone who stocks up on various items garnered through trade, then makes that stock available to others from one location. Buyers bring items to trade or use a medium of exchange, such as conch shells or (later) currency.

Third Generation—The *peddler* took his "store" on the road to hock his wares to new customers in new locations. This wandering vendor was the first "pitchman." The pitchman (or pitchwoman) is alive and well on cable TV, infomercials, and at the state fair. It seems the peddler's cart has been abandoned for air time.

Fourth Generation—When the peddler discovered the profit in repeat business, he began to follow a *route*. If you have a newspaper delivered on your doorstep or products delivered through the mail on a regular basis, you are a customer along the modern route.

Fifth Generation—The *"scientific" approach* began in 1939 with Dale Carnegie training. Sayings like "find a need and fill it" define this generation of selling. The underlying idea was that salespeople could find prospects who lacked the benefit the product provided and then convince them to buy it. This approach has always been product-driven, and often salespeople believe that *everyone* needs what they have to sell. Frequently called *needs selling* or *solution selling,* the scientific approach spawned the hook, features and benefits, objection handling, and closing skills. This is where memorization of scripts and techniques began. Salespeople who operate at this level spend a lot of time prospecting and marketing for new business.

Sixth Generation—Then came the *consultative approach.* Along the way, someone noticed that people would rather buy from a person they like, so "rapport building" was emphasized. The theory: Become their buddy, and they are more likely to buy from you. So consultative salespeople search for common ground and engage in chitchat to create feelings of rapport. Then they ask probing questions to put the prospect in a frame of mind where he or she is likely to accept the solution the consultant proposes. The primary motive is still to sell a specific product, and the information gathered is strictly for that purpose.

Like the Generation Five salesperson, the Generation Six salesperson spends a lot of time prospecting and marketing for new business.

Seventh Generation—Enter the *trusted advisor.* The process of the trusted advisor is one of discovery and meaningful human connection. He or she acts as facilitator to help potential clients discover what's important (values), articulate their goals, and benchmark where they are now. This discovery *on the part of the prospective client* sets the tone for a healthy business relationship to naturally and rapidly develop.

The key characteristic that distinguishes the Generation Seven trusted advisors from the Generation Six salespeople is that trusted advisors don't care if they make the sale or not. The trusted advisor is interested only in a complete client relationship, not in making a sale or two—no matter how large the sale. In fact, the trusted advisor frequently refers people who just want to buy a product to a salesperson. (This tends to baffle the salesperson on the receiving end of the referral.) While clients of trusted advisors tend to buy everything that is recommended, they do so without feeling sold because they really weren't.

As you can imagine, trusted advisors enjoy the highest compensation and the luxury of not having to prospect and market, because clients of trusted advisors naturally refer their friends, family, and colleagues.

Each of these generations typifies a certain kind of professional, and each is an improvement on the prior one. Each generation also typifies a certain kind of organization. Yet we are in a time of transition, and many "generations" of managers, insurance agents, investment representatives, and financial advisors can and do co-exist.

This brings up an issue on which we, the authors, have a slight difference of opinion. Up to this chapter, we have been in perfect accord as we have presented you with the attitude, methods, and strategies for becoming a high-trust leader. Our one point of departure is exactly how and when to assist all producers in making the leap into Generation Seven, where the entire organization is composed of full-service, trusted advisors.

Norman's Point of View

Let me be clear: I would love for every producer in America to develop into Generation Seven. Yet in a practical sense, I think there are mitigating factors. If you are as experienced in recruiting as I, no doubt you know that not every person you bring into your organization will be the ideal producer, mature and sophisticated in the ways of business. Many won't yet have the interpersonal relationship skills or the technique or the talent required to become an instant success. I view the seven generations not only as a historical evolution of selling; I believe they also parallel the evolution of the individual. In other words, when I bring new producers into the business, I wouldn't start them at seven. In fact, many are starting all over America and all over the world today at four, five, and six. They don't have a clientele; they don't know the business; they haven't been trained at all. We've got to choose the proper placement for the person, depending on the abilities and attitudes they have from the outset. What's more, I think market demographics help to determine how producers can sell. In a community where the most affluent members earn $50,000 a year, then I think that the Generation Five or Six techniques may be more appropriate starting point, although the goal can always be to graduate to Generation Seven.

In the long term, there's no question that moving to Generation Seven and a high-trust interrelationship (client-producer-leader) with less pressure and more caring, sharing, and compassion is the future. But to start there is not always possible because there are so many different kinds of managers in so many different places. Some are in small towns, some in big cities. Some are dealing with an affluent market, some with a low-income market. Some have only certain products in their portfolio, while some have a complete portfolio. Managers may have different levels of expertise and different kinds of resources to support them, as well as certain limitations imposed on them by the companies they represent. Some companies mandate specific sales presentations that would preclude a pure Generation-Seven approach.

There are about 150,000 agents in life insurance alone (never mind the mutual fund and investment business for a moment), and I'd estimate 130,000 are working at the Generation Five level. My experience tells me that you can't just toss aside fifth and sixth generation techniques, because they are how the product gets sold—*they work* for a vast majority of people in our business. And the manager's job, in a nutshell, is to make sure the product is sold. It is also to help the producer continue to evolve so that the practice of selling becomes both more rewarding for the producer and more profitable over the long term both for the company and the individual.

I see Generation Seven as the dream, the vision, the pot of gold at the end of the rainbow. It is already in practice for a number of illustrious producers who either have the good fortune of working with progressive, high-trust leaders or are in independent practice. The producer who makes it to Generation Seven gets to spend more time developing meaningful client relationships and improving financial skills. He or she also gets to spend less time prospecting and marketing, which is hard work no matter how much you love to sell.

For managers who are working with fifth and sixth generation producers, you can pat yourself on the back for moving your people up the ladder as far as you have. You have created an organization of professionals, not peddlers. Yet I challenge you, if you have not already, to consider the impact of elevating your entire team to a new level. As a high-trust leader, you owe it to the people you work with to provide them with all possible avenues to the highest levels of success, and there's no question in my mind where that path ultimately leads: the trusted advisor, or Generation Seven.

Bill's Point of View

Some leaders and companies are making the transition to Generation Seven right now. I hope to inspire you to do the same. But I recognize that some companies, like people, are destined to lead, while others will do what they have always done: follow.

Generations Five and Six are not bad; Generation Seven is just better. The enemy of the best is often the good. Don't let the good of these earlier generations keep you from enjoying the benefit of the best that Generation Seven has to offer. Frankly, I don't see a bright future for *salespeople* in financial services any more than Henry Ford saw much future for the horse and carriage. I doubt Henry was anti-horse. He was just really excited about the car.

You might remember when the financial needs analysis was a radical idea. You might remember when stock brokers swore they would never sell life insurance or become financial planners. You might remember when your insurance company would take away your contract if they caught you selling mutual funds. You might remember when banks did banking.

This is not your father's Oldsmobile.

Financial services is different. It's not like selling copy machines, real estate, or cell phones. Trusting your copy machine salesperson is a plus but not entirely necessary. Trusting your financial professional is an absolute necessity. And the reason sales techniques are a bad idea is that behaving like a salesperson causes people to *not* trust you. On the other hand, when you are trusted, you do not need anything you learned in sales training! So why is there still so much sales training and very little trust training? Good question.

It is true that some people are not capable of being Generation Seven trusted advisors. My advice: *Don't hire those people.*

It is true that some companies continue to mandate old school sales presentations and techniques. Have you noticed trusted advisors leaving those firms in droves?

Is recruiting easier or more challenging today? Does the mature adult contemplating a second or third career really want to become a product salesperson?

I am not criticizing anyone for being part of Generation Five or Six any more than I would criticize you for where you grew up. I "grew up" in Generation Five and Six, too. But let me remind you: One of our most important lessons is that what got us where we are today may not be the best thing to take us where we want to be in the future. I am, however, somewhat confused by people who would consciously choose to remain at the level of Generation Five or Six.

Can you teach a brand new person, young and inexperienced, to be a Generation Seven trusted advisor? Yes. We do it daily. In fact, many leaders who implement our material have told me that it's often easier to teach a new producer than a veteran how to be a trusted advisor. The veteran has old-school sales habits that are hard to break. The truth is we have success with rookies and veterans. It's just that the veterans sometimes take a little longer.

In our Trusted Advisor Coach™ program, we coach very successful producers—those veterans who have realized there must be a better way—through the transition from being great salespeople to becoming trusted advisors. They observe themselves on video tape artfully backing the prospect into the corner for the close. They see themselves digging the prospect a hole with questions clearly designed to disturb, create discomfort, or provide leverage to close the sale later. The Generation Five and Six salespeople tend to elicit negative emotions, such as fear, greed, and "love," which is actually fear of outliving your money, greed for a higher return, or guilt about not doing enough to provide security for those you love. Do these tactics work? Of course! Are salespeople bad people because they sell? Of course not! Yet in giving them a choice between being a salesperson or a trusted advisor, between sales training or trust training, I've never met anyone who chooses to be a salesperson.

Do your producers have a choice? Can you imagine how much easier it will be to *attract* producers to your organization if they are going to be

In the client's mind, the trusted advisor occupies a higher position.

developed into trusted advisors and not salespeople?

Being a trusted advisor isn't some soft, new-age mumbo jumbo or a matter of semantics. Trusted advisors produce big results. If results are measured by assets under management, insurance business that stays on the books, a clientele that consistently provides referrals, written financial plans, estate plans, charitable trusts, and investment policy statements that are implemented now, then the trusted advisor is seriously productive.

You are a successful leader. Now it's time for you to choose how you will be successful in the future. What got you to your current level of success may not be the best way to get to the next level of success. Can every organization belong to Generation Seven? Maybe not. So the question is what kind of organization *you* want to run. Will you lead salespeople or trusted advisors?

Putting It All Together: Going to the Next Level

How can you help your own organization and producers evolve, either immediately or over time? The first step is to become a high-trust leader yourself. Use what you've learned here to help you create the type of organization you can be proud of, and to recruit and train the type of producer you know you can help succeed. Next, teach high-trust client-relationship skills and not just old sales skills. Keep yourself up to date, and educate the powers that be in your company if necessary. Use the resources available to you and your producers.

The last thing you want to do as a producer-centered leader is to maintain the status quo strictly for your own comfort or because "it ain't broke." We encourage you to seriously evaluate your organization and your role in attracting the kind of producers you want, setting an example of the kind of relationship producers should aspire to, and protecting the organizational culture.

The natural result of a full-fledged Generation Seven organization is a team of highly paid trusted advisors with a totally loyal clientele which does all their prospecting and marketing for them. The trusted advisor tends to have a great quality of life, one that is balanced and full. The high-trust leader who heads this organization has the honor and satisfaction of helping producers achieve their version of the great life, and in the process creates his or her own, too. As a result, the recruiting process becomes less a matter of *push,* and one more of *pull:* Successful, progressive people will always work with successful, progressive leaders. This is what it means to "coach to win." Other people win, and so do you.

It's Not the Methods

We hope we've gotten you thinking about what *really influences* human behavior beyond your current approach to building long-term business relationships. Our ideas are not necessarily meant to replace your current strategy or system. They are designed to enhance it, to bring it to the next level.

The strength of leadership is not methodology; it's not the systems; it's not the procedures. All of those are normal parts of every organization and can assume many forms. Instead, it's the emotional commitment between the leader and the people with whom he or she works that creates high trust and a commitment to collaborate for a common cause. The bond is far stronger than just business or dollars.

In working with the financial services industry as speakers, trainers, and consultants, we get just a taste of what could be yours. There is nothing more rewarding than having leaders and producers tell us how our message has profoundly affected their lives. And it's not the amount of money they make or the sales awards they have won, although we hear about that, too. It is the quality of life they have achieved as a direct result of being involved in such a dynamic and rewarding industry. It is the difference they make in clients' lives, the longevity of their relationships. It is the pride they have in achieving their goals and dreams, and in living a life that honors their values. No doubt you've had moments like this with your producers, where they thank you sincerely for your guidance, patience, and sincere interest in their success. We'd be surprised if a reader of a book called *High-Trust Leadership* hadn't had at least one remarkable, memorable moment to reinforce what he or she already knows deep inside: It's the relationship that counts.

You now have a choice about what to make of the financial services industry tomorrow. The leaders of organizations are the most influential link in the entire system, setting the pace and the example of what is to come. Both the financial products companies and the producers depend on you. The whole system collapses without you. Without any question, the full evolution of the financial services industry will depend on great leaders who learn to create permanent, high-trust relationships with *producers* while maintaining a dignified relationship with the *companies* and *support people.*

A synergistic relationship between these three components is critical to building a great organization. You can't do it unless you get all three of them feeling that esprit de corps, that common bond.

Contrary to some people's perceptions, all three groups of people can build a lot of pride—and it can be *fun.* People can enjoy what they're doing. Imagine that! That's the secret of high-trust relationships: If you are nonadversarial and unconfrontational, if you recognize that each person is a whole person and respect all aspects of their individuality, you have the foundation of a truly great organization. Each person must know that you care not only about his or her career, but also the other "compartments" of life: family, health, time off, hobbies, etc. This builds pride, and yes, leads to having fun. Don't think of your organization as a "well-oiled machine"; this implies that people are only parts of the machine, and all you care about is whether they're working or not. Instead, consider your organization a dynamic community and culture with multiple dimensions and a life outside the office.

We'd like to tell you one last story to illustrate the point. It's a true story, yet because of its sensitive nature, we've changed certain details to maintain the anonymity of the people in it.

Two producers we know were fortunate to both be a part of the same high-trust organization. The leader knew them well, respected them, even loved them, having met their families and spent a good deal of social time with them. She had seen them through the early parts of their careers, coached them through the rough spots, and helped them attain great success by anyone's standards. One was in his thirties, the other in his fifties. By strange coincidence, they found out in the same month that they both had cancer.

Faced with this tremendous stress, the two reacted entirely differently. The older gentleman was given only a year to live—but never stopped living. He continued to attend all business functions (including social gatherings, where he was always the life of the party), was active in his college alumni group, took special trips with his friends, and began contributing regularly to causes he believed in. The younger fellow was given a less specific time period for his illness—his cancer went into remission shortly after it was discovered—yet he was so shaken that he retired from the business, and, for that matter, from the human race. He moved into God's waiting room. He broke off contact with his friends and closed himself up in his house in a deeply depressed state.

The older man, who had determined to live life to the fullest, actually lived for five more years—five wonderful, fulfilling years. The younger man is alive today with his cancer still in remission, not yet threatened by death but choosing to never again fully live.

Which of these two stories is the tragic one? In a business where we're concerned with living too long or dying too soon, with insuring our income in the case of disability and protecting our assets for our heirs, surely we all recognize the profound hardship that can come with illness and the inevitability of death. But how many of us, knowing that everybody will go when the time comes, really live? And how many of us just go from day to day, waiting until it's over?

The people we know who watched these two producers choose such very different paths all agree on one thing: If they had to choose living only a few more years—but living—or merely existing indefinitely, every one of us would have, without exception, opted for the few years of really living.

One of our charges as leaders is to help people fulfill their dreams, to find that thrill in living. You and your producers need something to be excited about, proud about, a vision for the future that starts today. You need the satisfaction of continuously pursuing and attaining those "Big, Hairy, Audacious Goals." You need the support and stimulation of genuine, caring relationships. You need each other.

Ask for the moon . . . Shoot for the stars!

Each of us has only one life to live. As we say good-bye for now, we have a simple wish for you: high-trust relationships with the producers and staff in your organization, and with everyone who is important to you. We wish you the honor of being a leader not only in your organization, but in your family, community, and the world at large. We believe you have the talent, and now you have the tools to be a High-Trust Leader.

About the Authors

Bill Bachrach, CSP is one of the foremost success resources for the financial services industry. Bill's personal success in our business is apparent in everything he teaches. His work has been instrumental in helping leaders and producers make the transition from transaction salespeople to full-service trusted advisors. Bill's best-selling book, *Values-Based Selling: The Art of Building High-Trust Client Relationships for Financial Advisors, Insurance Agents and Investment Reps* is considered a "must-read" book in our business. Since 1992 Bill has given over 500 presentations at some of the industry's most prestigious conferences, including multiple appearances at MDRT, IAFP, IIMC, and LAMP, as well as corporate and association conventions around the world.

Top producers invest $15,000 each to participate in his Trusted Advisor Coach™ program. His self-study video and audio learning systems and Values-Based Selling Academy are popular success tools for producers at all levels.

Bill's articles have appeared in over 75 financial services publications, and his column "The Trusted Advisor" is published monthly in *Ticker* magazine.

In 1998 Bill achieved a personal milestone by completing the Hawaii Ironman Triathlon. The 2.4-mile swim, 112-mile bike ride, and 26.2-mile marathon run, held every year in the rugged volcanic terrain of Hawaii's Big Island, is considered to be the toughest single-day athletic event in the world.

Bill lives in San Diego with his wife, Anne, who helped him build his business and was vital "support crew" on the training road to Ironman.

N ow a full-time speaker, motivator, trainer, and consultant, **Norman Levine, CLU, ChFC** works with companies and organizations around the world, helping them to improve productivity and effectiveness. He reflects the uniqueness of a practitioner who concurrently personally produced, ran a large agency, and volunteered in professional organizations while writing several books and speaking more than fifty times a year for more than forty years.

Norman is the only individual ever to have garnered all four of the highest honors of the life insurance industry: as a personal producer, he achieved the Million Dollar Round Table designation of "top of the table" and received the General Agents and Managers Association's (GAMA) highest award for productivity, "The Master Agency Award;" he has also been elected to GAMA's "Hall of Fame" and received the John Newton Russell Award. As a regular industry volunteer, Norman was the president of several of the major field organizations, including the National Association of Life Underwriters. He was also national president of GAMA and national chair of the Life Underwriters Training Council. He's been regional vice president of the Million Dollar Round Table and active in all other field organizations, as well.

Norman is the author of five books and many audio and video tapes sold worldwide. He has spoken in twenty-three countries and in all fifty states to audiences as large as fifteen thousand. One of the more illustrious venues has been the Million Dollar Round Table, an organization whose annual meeting is considered the hallmark of excellence by speakers all over the world. Norman has been on the main platform eight times and has led more than fifteen break-out sessions with this group.

His wife, Sandy, shares all aspects of his life: family, business, industry, community, and social. They live in Woodside, California and have three married children, Linda, Dan, and Don (all of whom chose to join the financial services industry) and five grandchildren.

Levine Enterprises Presents
The Levine "Formula"

A PRescription For Success

"Ingredients"

- In-person presentations
- Skill development and motivational books
- Audio and video training tapes

NORMAN G. LEVINE

THE LEVINE FORMULA

Norman G. Levine and Levine Enterprises are dedicated to helping companies and individuals achieve their personal and career dreams and aspirations.

Motivated people can reach their unrealized potential if they have dreams, which are converted into specific goals, which are then developed into realistic plans, which when implemented become building blocks in their chosen career path.

The Levine Formula is a proven plan for success and consists of three components which can be utilized by companies and individuals, separately or in combination, to effectively achieve career and personal objectives.

Each component can stand alone to raise performance levels, but to maximize the "Levine Formula's" potential, a coordinated program should be considered.

A COORDINATED PROGRAM

The program involves three steps:

STEP I

Norman Levine would do one or more in-person presentations.

STEP II

Each attendee would receive appropriate books to use as a guide and as a future reference source. The action projects should be implemented.

STEP III

A follow-up course would be provided using video presentations to the same participating group with a minimum of one-week intervals. Discussions would precede each session as to how the participants utilized the information in the preceding session. The participants could also receive a set of audio tapes of the video sessions to use as repeat refreshers until the materials become totally assimilated.

Though this three-step process is truly ideal, each component can contribute to one's growth and well-being and can be used separately.

"IN-PERSON" PRESENTATIONS

Norman Levine is available for in-person presentations. He has spoken worldwide for over 30 years to audiences as small as 10 and as large as 15,000. His proven effectiveness has, until now, resulted in the demand for his time exceeding his availability. However, he will be allocating more time for these activities in the future.

His primary topics are:

- Raising one's sights and expectations
- Motivation to raise expectations
- Management skills
- Time control techniques
- Sales skills

The formats utilized include:

- Individual speeches at company and industry meetings
- Half-day workshops to address specific issues
- Full- or multiple-day training sessions
- Scheduled multiple-visit training sessions over a period of time, usually a year or more.

As a very successful practitioner, while concurrently effectively sharing his ideas and motivating his audiences to achieving new heights of accomplishments, he is a unique success story among his motivational and training peers.

PUBLICATIONS

Four books are primarily appropriate for readers in the financial service industry. *Selling With Silk Gloves, Not Brass Knuckles* and the workbook are of universal interest.

FINANCIAL SERVICE BOOKS

The Norman Levine Reader

This book provides a multidimensional perspective of Norman Levine's career, including four essays excerpted from previously published books; a chronological presentation of eight platform speeches for MDRT in the 70s, 80s, and 90s; and a detailed first-person account of his illustrious career.

Yes You Can

A great "how to" sales book for all insurance and financial services salespeople. Available in English, Chinese and Thai.

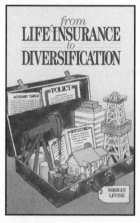

From Life Insurance to Diversification

A specialty book for life insurance salespeople and managers who want to diversify their financial product and service portfolio. Available in English only.

How to Build a $100,000,000 Agency in 5 Years or Less

A "how to" book for managers in the life insurance industry which includes specific information on sales agency building. Available in English, Chinese, and Thai.

SELF-IMPROVEMENT AND SALES SKILL MATERIALS OF GENERAL INTEREST

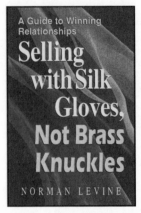

Selling With Silk Gloves, Not Brass Knuckles

A great sales book to help any reader raise their sights and dreams and then achieve them. Relationships are a prime key for success and/or happiness. This book shows how to develop winning relationships by using selling skills in your everyday life. This is a great book for anyone, whether in a sales career or not, who wants to be the best they can be. Available in English and Chinese.

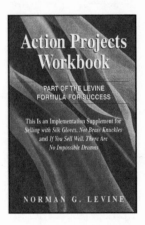

Action Projects Workbook

This is a composite of the action projects in *Selling With Silk Gloves, Not Brass Knuckles*. It allows followers of the "Levine Formula" to establish a plan of action and then to periodically measure their progress as they proceed toward achieving their dreams and aspirations. Available in English only.

AUDIO AND VIDEO CASSETTES

The third part of the Levine Formula is the tape programs. The video tapes can be utilized for multiple person audiences, either as single motivational presentations or as a series that is presented as a scheduled training course. The audio cassettes are best used by individuals as periodic refreshers or motivators for previously heard or seen methodologies, or to self-teach by using them as a training course. All the tapes are intended for business practitioners with an emphasis on sales and management. Some are primarily for insurance people and others are for any business persuasion.

FOR THE INSURANCE INDUSTRY:

- **"Live From England"** — A six-tape series of specific, skill-oriented motivational tapes. Available in audio and video versions.

- **"Rededication for Success"** — A single tape to help salespeople recharge their enthusiasm when they need a pick-up. Available in a single audio cassette.

- **"Basic Sales Skills — The Common Denominators of Success"** — A six-tape course on insurance selling skills which should be presented, one tape per week, over a six-week period. For multiple-person audiences, group discussions should precede and follow each tape session. Available in audio and video versions.

- **"High-Touch Management Skills"** — A four-tape series discussing many of the skills and methodologies necessary to build and expand a life insurance agency. Available in audio version.

FOR BUSINESS AND SALESPEOPLE OF ANY PERSUASION:

- **"If You Sell Well, There Are No Impossible Dreams"** — An eight-tape series covering many of the necessary skills and procedures to be the best you can be. It comes with a workbook to help the practitioner establish higher dreams and aspirations, set goals, make a plan, implement the plan, work effectively and become a world-class salesperson. Available in audio and video versions.

FOR MORE INFORMATION, PLEASE CONTACT:

Norman G. Levine
LEVINE ENTERPRISES
One California Street, Suite 300
San Francisco, CA 94111
Telephone: (800) 991-7281
Fax: (415) 391-6569
www.levineenterprises.com
norman@levineenterprises.com

Norman G. Levine, CLU, ChFC
Motivational and Sales Skills

ORDER FORM

Please photocopy this form and mail with your payment, or fax with your credit card information to our office.

Mail Orders : Levine & Associates, Inc.
One California Street, Suite 300 • San Francicso, CA 94111
Fax Orders : (415) 391-6569

Or you may purchase these items online at:
www.levineenterprises.com

TAPES

"If You Sell Well, There Are No Impossible Dreams" (set of 8 tapes)
includes bonus workbook!

_____ Set(s) Video (American VHS format) . . . .$399.95 each

_____ Set(s) Video (European PAL format) . . . .$399.95 each

_____ Set(s) Audio . . . .$79.95 each

"Basic Sales Skills — The Common Denominators of Success" (set of 6 tapes)

_____ Set(s) Video (American VHS format) . . . .$295.00 each

_____ Set(s) Video (European PAL format) . . . .$295.00 each

_____ Set(s) Audio . . . .$59.95 each

"Live from England" (set of 6 tapes)

_____ Set(s) Video . . . .$295.00 each

_____ Set(s) Audio . . . .$49.95 each

"High-Touch Management Skills" (set of 4 tapes)

_____ Set(s) Audio . . . .$54.95 each

"Rededication for Success" (single tape)

_____ Copy(s) Audio . . . .$15.00 each

• For video tapes, please add $10.00 per set for shipping and handling;
$5.00 per set for audio tapes. • California residents add 8.50% sales tax.

(continued next page)

BOOKS

_____ Copy(s) *High-Trust Leadership* ....$27.95 each

_____ Copy(s) *The Norman Levine Reader* ....$24.95 each

_____ Copy(s) *Selling With Silk Gloves, Not Brass Knuckles* ......$18.95 each
     ❏ English Edition   ❏ Chinese Edition

_____ Copy(s) *Yes You Can* ....$15.95 each
     ❏ English Edition   ❏ Thai Edition   ❏ Chinese Edition

_____ Copy(s) *From Life Insurance to Diversification* ....$15.95 each

_____ Copy(s) *Action Projects Workbook* ....$4.00 each

    • Please add $3.00 per book for shipping and handling.
      • California residents add 8.50% sales tax.
      • Discounts available for quantity purchases.

International Orders

Please use the following information for shipping and handling
charges on international orders:
VIDEO: Air Mail $48.00 — Sea Mail $24.00
AUDIO: Air Mail $18.00 — Sea Mail $12.00
BOOKS: Air Mail $12.00 — Sea Mail $6.00

Please Select Payment Method

❏ Check (payable to **Norman G. Levine & Associates**) Total enclosed $_____
❏ MasterCard ❏ Visa

Account Number:_____ Expires:_____

Signature: _____
     (signature required for credit card orders)

Name: _____

Business Name: _____

Company Affiliation: _____

Address: _____

City State ZIP _____

Telephone: _____

Mail Orders : Levine & Associates, Inc.
One California Street, Suite 300 • San Francicso, CA 94111
Fax Orders : (415) 391-6569

About Bachrach & Associates, Inc.

Since 1988, **Bachrach & Associates, Inc.** has been providing leading-edge speaking, training, consulting and coaching services exclusively for the financial services industry. Through Bill Bachrach's Values-Based Selling programs, financial advisors, insurance agents and investment reps learn specific skills and methods to purposefully and rapidly gain client trust, get clients emotionally committed to make smart financial choices and ethically influence them to act now. Leaders and managers in the financial services industry use these same skills in recruiting and building high-performance teams.

Due to the impact of Values-Based Selling and the power of Bill Bachrach's presentation style, many top firms not only request him as a speaker for all their meetings, but they also engage Bachrach & Associates, Inc. for consulting and training to create complete client development and recruiting systems consistent with values-based relationships.

Bachrach & Associates, Inc. provides keynote presentations, training and consulting services, audio- and video-based learning systems, books and top-producer coaching. All these services are designed to assist individuals and companies in the financial services industry to achieve even greater success through building high-trust relationships with clients as well as within the company. For more information, please see the order form in the back of this section, visit our website at **www.bachrachvbs.com** or call (800) 347-3707.

8380 Miramar Mall, Suite 233
San Diego, CA 92121
Tel. (800) 347-3707
Fax (619) 558-0748
E-mail: info@bachrachvbs.com
http://www.bachrachvbs.com

Values-Based Selling: The Art of Building
High-Trust Client Relationships for Financial Advisors, Insurance Agents and Investment Reps

In this breakthrough book written specifically for financial advisors, insurance agents, and investment representatives, industry pacesetter Bill Bachrach gives producers a step-by-step plan for building the high-trust client relationships that will take them, you, and your business to the next level—no matter where you are currently.

An Industry Bestseller and a Vital Resource for Any High-Trust Organization

Only $34.95

What Leaders and Top Producers Say About This "Must-Read":

"It should be mandatory for anybody new in the business, and it should be read and reviewed continually by veterans."
        —**Donald A. Connelly** • Sr. Vice-President & Sr. Key Account Manager, Putnam

"A doctor client of mine gave me $1.35 million in rollover money, bought a $1 million survivor policy, a $1 million term policy and entrusted me wiht many other financial decisions when he retired—all because of your Values-Based Selling system. He has also referred me to five other doctors who will retire within five years."
        —**Tom Tessier**, "Top of the Table" Member • Weisman & Tessier Associates

"As a result of implementing your Values-Based Selling process, I have tripled my business in one year. I now have people calling me who want to do business with me."
        —**Jay Paterson** • Vice-President of Sales, Capital Management Group

"Very interesting! This book is a perfect road map for how to succeed in the financial services industry today and in the foreseeable future."
        —**William W. Fenniman** • CEO & President, Hemisphere Group

Values Conversation and Financial Road Map Training Videos

If a picture is worth a thousand words, these video tapes can be worth hundreds of thousands of dollars. There's nothing more powerful than watching the master in action.

On these $3^{1}/_{2}$ hours of video tapes, Bill demonstrates every situation you will encounter on your way to taking great client relationships to the highest possible level. Bill Bachrach demonstrates the Values Conversation with:

- *couples, both pre-retirement and financially independent*

Only $97 each!

- *business owners, both sole proprietors and partners*
- *successful women*
- *successful "driver" types*

Bill will show you how to turn apparently difficult situations into golden opportunities.

You will also see two demonstrations of the entire Financial Road Map interview with a pre-retirement "baby-boomer" couple and a wealthy retired couple, from the opening of the meeting to getting the check.

These videos will dramatically accelerate your understanding and mastery of the Values Conversation and the Financial Road Map.

Mail or fax us the reply form in the back of this section or call (800) 347-3707 to purchase.

Success Road Map and Financial Road Map
Vital Tools for Inspiring Action

The value of a compelling visual representation of values, goals and current financial reality cannot be underestimated.

The **Success Road Map** is available in a 17" x 22" version for desktop use—producers can keep the original and the leader can keep a copy in the file. The back includes the 9 Core Competencies and planning worksheet.

PRICE $29 FOR PACKAGE OF 25 MAPS.

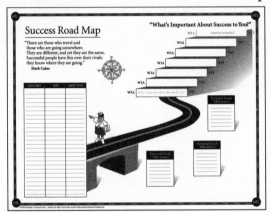

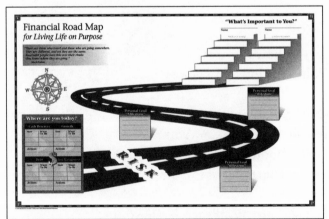

Featured in *Values-Based Selling,* the **Financial Road Map** is available as a big (27" x 39") laminated poster for use with erasable markers.

It's ideal for client meetings and presentations. PRICE $79.

Also available in a 17" x 22" version for desktop use with simple fact-finder on the back. PRICE $29 FOR PACKAGE OF 25 MAPS.

Call (800) 347-3707 now for a free sample, or mail us the reply form in the back of this section to purchase.

The Winning Spirit
A Book of Championship Caliber

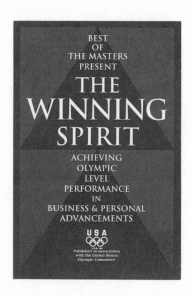

"If your profession were an Olympic event, would you make the team?" Bill Bachrach asks in the first chapter of this extraordinary book of short essays by 20 of the country's finest motivational speakers. Inspired by the determination, spirit and will of Olympic athletes, *The Winning Spirit* considers these same qualities in terms of daily life. In addition to Bill Bachrach's essay, "Olympic Thinking," contributions include

- Jim Tunney on "Mental Biceps,"
- Tony Alessandra on "Take Aim in Life,"
- George Walther on "Win the Gold With Mettle,"
- Bill Brooks on "How to Be Your Own Coach,"
- Jim Cathcart on "Helping People Grow,"
- Les Brown on "Olympic Dreams."

The Winning Spirit was published in association with the United States Olympic Committee. PRICE $16.95

Mail or fax us the reply form in the back of this section or call (800) 347-3707 to purchase.

Values-Based Selling Academy

A Three-Day Learning Experience for Producers and Leaders at All Levels to Master the Financial Road Map or Success Road Map

In this highly interactive learning experience, producers are taught and see demonstrations of the Values Conversation and Financial Road Map, then role play and practice what they've learned. It is a three-day immersion in the interviewing and presentation skills that are the cornerstones of Values-Based Selling. Producers can expect to walk away from the course with absolute clarity about the attitudes and process that will make every client interview a success.

Mail or fax us the reply form in the back of this section or call (800) 347-3707 for further information or to enroll today.

The Trusted Advisor Coach—

A One-Year Coaching Experience Exclusively for Top Producers and Leaders Who Seek to Perfect Their Interview Skills

Professional and Olympic athletes have very specific formulas and coaching to make small adjustments in their actions, which translate into huge gains in their performance. Using similar strategies, you can unlock your true potential for building high-trust client relationships. But where can you get the coaching necessary to make this happen? Until now, nowhere.

Isn't it time you did?

To qualify, you must

- show proof of a personal annual income in excess of $100,000,

- be open to frank evaluation of your skills,

- be very good at the client interview right now,

- be familiar with Values-Based Selling,

- have big goals and a secure ego.

Big goals means income in excess of $250,000, $500,000, $1,000,000 or more. It means two to four months per year of free time. It means a quality of life that includes total goal achievement and values fulfillment. It means truly making a difference in the lives of others.

> *"The insights I took away from this initial meeting will be worth many millions of dollars to me."*
> **Mark Pace,** CLU, RHU, ChFC
> Achates Companies

(continued next page)

A MESSAGE FROM BILL BACHRACH

"Nothing is more effective for discovering what you are truly made of than seeing yourself on video tape and listening to yourself on audio tape.

There's no place to hide and not everybody can handle it. Even some top-producers prefer to hide from the truth rather than confront it, learn from it, and raise their game to the next level. My coaching program is for top-producers who want to discover the truth and use it as a benchmark to pursue perfection. Perfection may never be achieved, but it's the only worthy goal of the elite performer. I find it remarkable that successful financial professionals are more likely to have video taped their golf swing than their client interview.

This program provides a unique environment, a powerful year of coaching, and the added benefit of being with a small group of your peers who are as committed as you to being the best."

- BILL BACHRACH

"Since completing The Trusted Advisor Coach program in 1997 and implementing the strategies you teach, I doubled my income in 1997 and I am on track to double my income again this year!"

Dennis R. Fletcher
Fletcher Financial Network

"A prospect from my seminar came to my office intending to open a $10,000 account. Because I had attended the Trusted Advisor Coach program and used Values-Based Selling, he left the first meeting giving me almost $1,000,000 in assets instead. And that's just one of the many success stories I could tell about implementing what you teach."

David Bach
Morgan Stanley Dean Witter

Because there are few resources and little support in the financial services industry for people who choose to operate at your level, The Trusted Advisor Coach is an exclusive skill development process designed specifically for you. There are no gimmicks or cute techniques. Just smart work, intense coaching, lots of feedback and real-world application. Using the strategies of elite athletes and interaction with your peers, you will move to a level most financial professionals can't even imagine.

Tuition: $15,000

Enrollment by personal interview with
Bill Bachrach only.

Mail or fax us the reply form in the back of this section or call (800) 347-3707 for further information or to apply today.

BACHRACH & ASSOCIATES PRODUCT ORDER FORM

THESE ITEMS ARE INCLUDED IN THE MASTERY SYSTEM (vertical text at left)

ITEM (Volume discounts available on all items—call for details)	QTY	UNIT PRICE	TOTAL
The Mastery System Get it all, and save over $100!		~~$512.90~~ **$399.**00	
Values Conversation Training Video 90 minutes of Values Conversation demonstrations		$97.00	
Financial Road Map Training Video 2 hours of Financial Road Map demonstrations		$97.00	
Values-Based Selling Audio Cassette Series 8+ hours on 8 audio tapes		$159.00	
Values-Based Selling book		$34.95	
Financial Road Map (22" x 17") Package of 25, paper, for desktop use		$29.00	
Financial Road Map (39" x 27") Laminated poster for use with dry erasable markers		$79.00	
The Winning Spirit book Opening chapter by Bill Bachrach, published in association with the U.S. Olympic Committee		$16.95	
High-Trust Leadership book		$27.95	
Success Road Map (22" x 17") Package of 25, paper, for desktop use		$29.00	
SUBTOTAL			
7.75% SALES TAX (California residents only)			
SHIPPING & HANDLING (See chart)			
TOTAL All funds U.S. dollars		$	

BACHRACH
 & ASSOCIATES • INC
 Values-Based Selling

To order call
(800) 347-3707,
visit our website at
www.bachrachvbs.com,
or photocopy
this form and mail to:

Bachrach & Associates
8380 Miramar Mall,
Suite 233
San Diego, CA 92121

— or fax to —

(619) 558-0748.
Thank You!

U.S. SHIPPING & HANDLING

(call for charges outside U.S. or to expedite shipping):

Orders are shipped
UPS GROUND.

For orders	
up to $50	$ 5.00
$51–$100	$10.00
$101–$300	$15.00
$301–500	$25.00
Over $500 call for price	

If you desire express delivery, please call us for assistance. International shipping additional. Does not include customs or brokerage fees.

❏ **Here's my check** (payable to Bachrach & Associates, Inc.).
Please charge my: ❏ American Express ❏ Visa ❏ MasterCard ❏ Discover

Card # _____ Expires _____

Signature _____

Name _____

Company _____

Address _____

City _____ State _____ Zip _____

Phone ( ) _____ Fax ( ) _____

e-mail _____

I'd like to know more! Please call me about
❏ customized keynote speeches or workshops
❏ on-site training and consulting services
❏ The Values-Based Selling Academy
❏ The Trusted Advisor Coach program for top producers